WEST LAFAYETTE PUBLIC LIBRARY

3 1951 003⬛ ⬛⬛⬛

S0-BZB-177

WITHDRAWN

THIS BOOK IS A GIFT FROM

THE FRIENDS OF THE WEST LAFAYETTE PUBLIC LIBRARY

2011

A BOOK IS A TREASURE TO OPEN AGAIN AND AGAIN

378.125 KLO
Klose, Robert
  The three-legged woman &
other excursions in teaching

9/11

West Lafayette Public Library
West Lafayette, Indiana

the three-legged woman
& other excursions in teaching

ALSO BY ROBERT KLOSE

Adopting Alyosha —
   A Single Man Finds a Son in Russia

Small Worlds —
   Adopted Sons, Pet Piranhas
   & Other Mortal Concerns

the three-legged woman
& other
excursions in
teaching

ROBERT KLOSE

UNIVERSITY PRESS OF NEW ENGLAND

♣ Hanover and London

West Lafayette Public Library
West Lafayette, Indiana

University Press of New England
www.upne.com
© 2010
University Press of New England
All rights reserved
Manufactured in the
United States of America
Designed by Eric M. Brooks
Typeset in Whitman and Block by
Passumpsic Publishing

University Press of New England is a
member of the Green Press Initiative.
The paper used in this book meets
their minimum requirement for
recycled paper.

For permission to reproduce
any of the material in this book,
contact Permissions, University Press
of New England, One Court Street,
Suite 250, Lebanon NH 03766;
or visit www.upne.com

Library of Congress
Cataloging-in-Publication Data
Klose, Robert.
The three-legged woman and other
excursions in teaching / Robert Klose.
    p. cm.   9/11 Amazon 16.55
ISBN 978-1-58465-927-3 (cloth :
alk. paper)
ISBN 978-1-58465-952-5
(electronic file)
1. College teaching — Maine —
Bangor. 2. Klose, Robert. 3. College
teachers — Maine — Bangor —
Biography. 4. University College
(Bangor, Me.) — Faculty —
Biography. I. Title.
LB2331.K56   2010
378.1'25097413 —
dc22   2010020780

5 4 3 2 1

Excerpt from "Personal Helicon"
from *Opened Ground: Selected Poems
1966–1996* by Seamus Heaney.
Copyright © 1998 by Seamus Heaney.
Reprinted by permission of Farrar,
Straus and Giroux, LLC.

The following pieces first appeared,
in shorter form, in *The Christian
Science Monitor*: "A Season for
Seaweeds," "I Rock," "Let Us Praise
the Bold Molds," "The Truth Is in the
Tape," "What I Say and What They
Hear," "Whoa Is the State of English."
"The Three-Legged Woman and The
Imp of the Paranormal" first appeared
in *Phi Delta Kappan* as "Atoms vs. a
Three-Legged Woman?"
"The Skeptic" is reworked from a
piece that first appeared in the *Bangor
Daily News* titled "Martian Life? Ye of
Too Much Faith."
"The Illiterati" was first published,
in shorter form, in the *Times Record*
(Brunswick, Maine) as, "Where Have
All the Readers Gone?"

♠ *In Memory of My Father*

contents

introduction

As per the title of the opening essay of this collection, I teach at a small, impoverished, careworn college. This signifies two things: one, that we are a threat to nobody and therefore are pretty much left alone to do what we do best (teach); and two, that open admissions is a necessity if we are to survive as an institution. The result is that my school has a fascinating—and often very challenging—mix of students. In my own classes they have ranged in age from seventeen to seventy-two. There have been students quivering with fear who do amazingly well, the overconfident who cannot comprehend the poverty of their performance, and the rabid overachievers for whom an A is a matter of life and death. I have taught the homeless, the abused, single parents, the unwitting, the witting, the well prepared and those seriously ill-equipped to go to college, the bright and not-so-bright, and the conflicted who put more energy into excuses for their absences and missed assignments than they do into the coursework itself (see my chapter, "The Death of Fiction"). I even once had a murderer in my class, who was otherwise a very nice person.

Teaching college is like being in the military in peacetime: no calls to battle stations, but a surfeit of ongoing intrigues. I try to run the gamut of them here, reflecting on such things as the decline of reading for enjoyment (and the resulting inability to interpret figurative text); the misbegotten belief that everyone must go to college (with predictably frustrating results for many); the ongoing challenge of teaching evolution, more than eighty years after the Scopes Monkey Trial was thought to have been the final catharsis; the folly of regarding e-mail as praiseworthy ersatz for expository writing; as well as some reflective essays on the profound joys of teaching, which can still be had in an age when teachers are under fire for presumably not working hard enough.

In sum, this collection represents the personal ruminations of one biology professor on the experience of teaching non-majors in a nondescript, out-of-the-way place which is more an outpost than a campus. It is a special vocation, and though teaching is no longer as respected as once upon a time, it still provides rewards that are absent in most other professions. It is, for sure, an imperfect occupation, as it is difficult if not impossible to get an entire class of students to rise to one's expectations. It is important, then, to do one's best; but equally important not to be shackled to the results of one's efforts, which might produce a depressing book. Teaching is, to say the least, an interesting ride, and this collection contains the truth, so far as I know it, of my experiences.

the three-legged woman
& other excursions in teaching

✯ ✯ ✯ ✯ ✯ ✯ ✯ ✯ ✯ ✯ ✯ ✯ ✯ ✯ ✯ ✯ ✯

my small, impoverished, careworn college

My school was once a military base, and this shows in the austere, blocky architecture of its widely spaced buildings. Spring and summer add a gloss of green to the desolation, but fall and especially winter are almost unbearably bleak. Think Murmansk, the industrial New Jersey waterfront (minus the water), or Chernobyl (without the glow).

I plod across the blank field separating the building that houses my office from another in which I teach. The wind screaming in from the nearby airport tarmac cuts, in the poet John Masefield's words, "like a whetted knife." I pull my collar closed, flex my fingers for warmth, lean forward and press on.

Actually, things have been looking up. At least a bit. For years we were little more than a "feeder" college for the—compared to us—mammoth University of Maine at Orono, eight miles up the road, with which we were associated. We received, by and large, the "rejects" who were not admitted to UM, and here they seethed, marinating in their resentment for not being allowed to matriculate as engineering students with their combined 700 SAT scores. Some of them kept a hand in at UM, taking one or two courses "up there," riding, between campuses, a yellow shuttle bus they had bitterly dubbed the "loser cruiser." Those who managed to eke out acceptable GPAs eventually transferred to UM. In the meantime, the bigger school skimmed off our tuition dollars, viewing us more or less as a cash cow for its general fund.

Truth to tell, nobody has ever known what to do with my campus. It had its inception in 1969 when the military vacated the base and turned the land over to the university. By default, we became the "South Campus of the University of Maine," or SCUM, and later, Penobscot Valley Community College, then Bangor Community College, and most recently University College. In

1

1998 the University of Maine, in a political move, disgorged us and our thousand students into the gullet of the University of Maine at Augusta, eighty miles to our south, ostensibly to pump up their flagging enrollment.

The last ten or so of those first twenty-eight years constituted what a Soviet citizen would call the "period of stagnation." Little to nothing was invested in the campus's infrastructure—I don't recall even a flower being planted. Once, when a window broke, we had to turn, hat-in-hand, to the University of Maine, which instructed us to find a piece of plywood. No wonder the students felt enervated, demoralized, neglected. They had come to us to learn, but divided their time between listening to the lectures and holding their coat collars closed while the frigid wind howled through poor-sealing windows, the radiators clanged, and paint peeled from the walls in sheets. In addition, alcoholics from the nearby residential treatment facility roamed the campus by night, looking for cans and bottles, and potholes as deep as watering troughs snapped the occasional axle. My office was in one of the old, squat, flat-roofed military administration buildings. The windows rattled in their frames, so in the winter ice crept in and coated the sills. In the summer the heat slowed my computer to a slog.

Still, there was a certain romance. The kind that is kindled when one is prevailing against the odds. I had my own little corner; my metal, government-issue desk; my metal, erector-set bookshelves; and a hotpot for my tea. I worked at my courses, did some writing, came and went as I pleased, and almost never saw the dean of the campus, who was ensconced like the Wizard of Oz behind his curtain in a building far removed from mine, dreaming ahead to a university presidency that, alas, would never come to be.

Another part of the charm was generated by a veteran faculty, many of whom had been teaching since the school's beginning (in other words, when I was still in high school). I arrived in 1986 and in fairly quick time realized why there was relatively little turnover. It was because neglect has a flip side that is very seductive: we were left alone to do the thing we did best — teach. In short, if I wanted to do something — create a new course, arrange a field trip, make a piece of scientific equipment from a found item at the dump, drill a hole in a wall — the philosophy was that it was easier to apologize later than to ask permission. Expectations for the faculty were few — teach a couple of courses and keep track of your advisees. No research responsibilities, no grants to write, no pressure to join committees, and only the occasional meeting. Now and then I published an article about teaching or politics or nature, which garnered me so much mileage in the approbation of colleagues and the administration that everyone seemed to redouble their efforts to *Leave Me Alone*. In short, I had the perfect job: it was as close as I could come to not working and still getting paid.

One day a professor from another campus of the University of Maine system paid an unannounced visit to my office. He said he knew me by reputation (this unnerved me, as I had done my best to keep my head down). The professor was one of those who had been teaching college since receiving his bachelor's degree. Now approaching sixty, he was thinking of retirement but also in terms of a few last hurrahs. In other words, he had some dreams left, mostly concerning the application of new technologies to outreach programs in prisons and high schools.

In truth, I've always been suspicious when someone approaches me with dreams, because dreams are followed by plans, and plans require meetings and paperwork. My fear is that, if I raise my profile by participating in any new initiatives, I will no longer be left alone. I will have to — gulp — *collaborate*. Perhaps submit reports. And maybe even sit on a — I can barely write the word — committee.

The thing is, I respect and appreciate people with ideas and the drive to precipitate them into reality. In this light, I listened to my colleague as he described a program that would allow designated professors to beam courses to high schools so that the students there could earn advance college credits. It would also, of course, be a way to improve the image of University College and let high schoolers know that we existed.

I had, in fact, once taught high school. In New Jersey. At an all-boys prep. I was a fresh-faced twenty-two-year-old, just out of college, with stars in my eyes. My enthusiasm and idealism made me a "Dead Poets Society" kind of teacher. I had enjoyed that year so much—despite the antics of my charges and the barriers to real learning they so often presented—that, at the end of the term, I did the counterintuitive: I left. Because I felt that if I stayed another year, I might never leave, and there were other doors I still wanted to open.

I think it was this recollection of a warm and happy high school teaching stint that seduced me into agreeing to work with the visiting professor. Besides, teaching over television would place a protective buffer between me and the high schoolers. I wouldn't have to deal with discipline, or even attendance. Those things would be handled, I presumed, by the high school. The professor asked me to put together an outline for a biology course. "It would be great if you could get it to me by morning."

"Morning?"

"Yes. Then I'll put it in our package and we can arrange to go to one of the schools."

Like a cornered animal I did what I had to do. I rose to the occasion and actually cobbled together a syllabus. A few days later we drove the thirty-five miles to the high school, were enthusiastically received by faculty and administrators, praised for our ideas, and then—nothing. The school didn't follow through, my professor friend became disillusioned, and I went back to my ice palace and the screaming of jet turbines in the distance.

Over the last ten years our environment has improved. A bit of money has been thrown at the campus and some of the buildings have been renovated. Although in winter we still resemble the tundra, trees have been planted, softening the campus's profile, at least during the warmer months. And our students, rather than being defaulted to us by other institutions, now apply directly to University College. Almost all are so-called non-traditional students, with families and work and a multitude of personal issues, some of which have been singular. I once taught a biology seminar with about ten students. During my introduction to the course I paused to ask them what they did in real life. One man was a police officer. There was a single mom with two young children. Another woman was returning to school to improve her job prospects. In the front row sat a fortyish man with a striking resemblance to Errol Flynn. "What about you?" I asked. Without batting an eye he said, "I'm a murderer."

I would say that the ensuing silence was deafening if not for my reluctance to use clichés. Be that as it may, I discovered that the fellow was, indeed, a murderer (he had deliberately run down another man with his truck), but received prison release time to take my class. When I asked him how he had heard of the course he said, "Your reputation." Once again, it was clear I wasn't lying low enough.

This points up an interesting, to say the least, aspect of teaching at an open admissions college: it's like running a literary magazine that pays only in copies — one never knows what's going to come in over the transom. This means that the classes have all sorts of characters. For some of the students the material is self-evident and they sail right along. Others are bright but have to work for their A's and B's. And then there are those who cannot connect with the subject matter and whose goal is a passing grade, however low. This requires that, as a teacher, I be nimble in the extreme. No class-encompassing assumptions about approach or student comprehension are possible.

For example, I was once giving a lecture on ecosystems. Some of my most capable students barely took notes: they were enjoying the ride, nodding, and adding their comments and questions at appropriate junctures. Then I mentioned a new concept — "biome" — that I defined as "a large, terrestrial ecosystem." Examples would be a desert or a pine forest. A tentative hand went up from a young woman in the back of the room. "I don't understand the term," she said. So I repeated myself. "A biome is an ecosystem," I elaborated. "But it's strictly applied to a terrestrial setting."

She shook her head. "Not that," she said. "What does 'terrestrial' mean?"

Then there was the thirtyish man who punctuated my every utterance with an editorial comment of his own, treating my class like a call and response revival. I finally took him aside and alerted him to the problem. "I can't stop talking," he explained. "The doctors are mystified." So I asked him what the solution was. "If I talk out of turn," he confided, "just give me a signal and I can suppress it." It turned out that, in addition to his unidentified malady, this man was severely dyslexic, but articulate and sharp. I did as he suggested, waving my hand at waist-level whenever he started to speak out of turn. We found our mutual grooves in the class, and I wound up reading the tests to him in my office because he couldn't make sense of the questions by himself.

These days academic life is sweet. I even serve on a committee, but was careful to choose one with a limited lifespan (unlike the frighteningly named "Committee on Committees," the Hades of eternal sinecures). But the 'sun' about which I orbit are my biology students, who continue to make life interesting. When I went into teaching, the mother of one of my friends made the rather snobbish observation that teaching struck her as repetitive and déclassé (her own son went into accounting). Although at the time I was at a loss for words, I now have years of teaching experience behind me and am ready and willing to state, first, that it is not repetitive. As each new semester approaches, I look forward to new students because every class has its own personality. There have been some groups with which I've really clicked, and others where the teaching was like pulling teeth. But part of the allure of teaching is the symbiosis between teacher and students, and the sense of anticipation that is part and parcel of the turning of the semesters: one never knows what the next cast of characters will bring.

As for that "déclassé" comment, I understand where it came from. An outside observer of classroom culture might think, at times, that the teacher is there for crowd control more than anything else. Of course, high school is far more prone to shenanigans than college. And sometimes I do allow things to get crazy, because there are moments—especially when the course material is particularly challenging—when both teacher and student need a break. If the mother of a dutiful accountant were to wander into my classroom when I was blowing things up or spreading shark guts out in a dissection tray, I would understand if she wrinkled her nose in derision.

And so I go on. Someone once pointed out to me that mine was the poorest college in the country. So what of it? I am reminded of what the Italian film director Roberto Benigni said when he received an Oscar for *Life Is Beautiful*. He thanked his parents for the gift of poverty. The well-heeled audience laughed. But they had missed his point. He wasn't trying to be funny. He was saying that poverty made him what he was, that his ideas were drawn from the well of his family's misfortunes. In other words, his was a déclassé world of colorful characters and austerity and endless dramas.

I could have called him colleague.

clientele

what happens if you step on it?

Every teacher has "times."

Times when he is not sure he is getting through.

Times when students repeatedly ask the same question because no one is listening.

Times when the students don't seem to be learning concepts that are eminently learnable.

Times when lack of attendance burdens teacher as well as students with the onus of incomplete work.

Such moments call for a fresh start, a clean slate; in other words, some form of renewal.

I have found such reinvigoration in the talks I occasionally give to our youngest students in the elementary schools, as when I was once asked to speak to a roomful of first graders. The topic: Sea Creatures.

I savored the opportunity to speak off the cuff without having to prepare anything resembling a lecture. And so I pulled together my specimens: octopi and crabs encased in plastic blocks; a plaster model of a lamprey eel; a dried-out sea urchin; the actual saw from a sawfish . . . All of them went—plop!—into the box until I had a grab bag of curiosities.

There were about thirty munchkins in the group. I could feel the heat of their enthusiasm as I approached the room. One of their teachers, Mrs. White, had managed to corral them into their desks and was gently instructing them on how to behave during my presentation. To no avail. When I appeared in the doorway with my box, they jumped to their feet and swamped me. I felt like a long-lost relative from the old country. They were all over me, their hands in the box, grabbing my arms, begging for attention. One little girl pleaded incongruously, "My father fixes pipes!"

I threw Mrs. White a helpless glance and she quickly interceded. The kids were soon sitting on their little bottoms again, but were by no means glued to the floor. They bounced for recognition, waving their hands desperately for a chance to speak.

After a short preamble, I proceeded to see how much general knowledge about marine life these kids had, so I could get a feeling for their level of understanding. After all, most of them were only six years old. And so I posed the question, "Can anybody name a sea creature that's not a fish?"

Every hand went up, each one punctuated with the word, "Me!" It was a sea of "me"s. "Me! Me! Oh, *please!* Me!"

I gathered myself for inevitable answers like "rock" and "hippopotamus," finally calling on a little boy in the back of the room. "Do you have one?" I asked.

He stood up and declared, "Zooplankton!"

Whoa. I had clearly underestimated my clientele. Okay, then. Let's go on to the specimens. I reached into my box of tricks and pulled out a preserved sea urchin. Once again, every hand shot up ("Oh, me! Me!"). Struggling to make my points against the exertions of the straining mass before me, I described the urchin's anatomy, where it was found, and its habits. "Any questions?" I asked.

I acknowledged a little girl in the front row. "Yes?"

She stared in wonder at the urchin and asked, "What happens if you step on it?"

"Well," I said, "it has spines, so you could hurt your foot."

The next specimen, a juvenile dogfish shark, elicited nigh pandemonium. After my comments I once again solicited questions. A little boy with a dense mask of freckles asked, "What happens if you step on it?"

I glanced at Mrs. White with faux exasperation. "You'll hurt your foot," I said, "because this shark has a spine on its fin."

And so the pattern was set. Specimen after specimen, from jellyfish to mussels to hermit crabs, the most pressing question was, "What happens if you step on it?"

I finally held my hand up and pronounced a dictum for a change of direction. "Okay, my friends, we've finished with asking what happens if you step on it. Our challenge now is to think of a new question to ask. All right?"

Nods all around.

I reached into my box and pulled out a magnificent preserved skate in a large, flat block of plastic. Oohs and aahs. Once again, after describing the creature, I asked for questions. Once again, all hands went up. At this point, some students were so weak from waving that they were supporting one arm with the other. I pointed to a boy who seemed particularly desperate. "Do you have a question?" I asked.

"Yes!"

Before I let him go on, I preempted him with, "Now, you're not going to ask me what happens if you step on it, are you?"

"No," he said, with an aggressive shake of his head.

"All right, then, what's your question?"

His response was immediate: "What happens if you *sit* on it?"

I have related this rather long-winded anecdote—every word of which is true—to make a point, or more accurately, to pose a question of my own, to wit: what happens to students between the ages of seven and, say, fifteen or sixteen, when they are embedded in high school? At age seven learning is an adventure. Eight years later, it becomes a chore, which attitude persists into the college classroom. I think there are several reasons for this.

One. At seven children are still tightly tied to the home, and the only other place they go with regularity is school, where almost everything is different. New. This creates a sense of anticipation, which most elementary school teachers are able to exploit to everyone's advantage (Teacher: "Tomorrow, class, we're going to make crystals." Students: "Yay!")

Two. The elementary schools task kids with producing beautiful products. Think of all those backpacks filled with artwork, jumbo spelling letters, writing journals with hand-drawn, personalized covers, science models, and math puzzles. When one is actually creating something, it fosters a sense of purpose, direction, and accomplishment. A child can point to the wall or a shelf and say, "This is my work. This is me."

Three. Little kids are recipients of the steady message that school is something they really need if they want to grow up to be "big and smart," "an astronaut," etc. And being at an age where they believe what they are told, they integrate this faith into most of their endeavors and proceed apace.

Now look at high schoolers in the context of these three tenets.

First point. Whereas a young child orbits almost exclusively the twin stars of home and school, a teenager's elliptic is significantly wider. It stretches well beyond home and high school to include all the—let's face it, the word is "superficial"—seductions of American popular culture. And in an age of essentially unlimited capital and unlimited "stuff," the desire to partake is stoked to white heat. Television, computers, videos, iPods, DVDs, iPhones, parties, alcohol, tobacco, drugs. There's a lot out there, and all of it—*all* of it—is designed to titillate the senses. How can school, with its predictable offerings of math, literature, and social sciences, ever hope to compete with those things that have been labeled "cool"? In many, many minds, it can't. Compared with what lies beyond academic corridors, school's a drag, man. This is why those kids who are "into" their studies are often viewed by their peers as hopelessly dysfunctional.

Second point. High school students, by and large, do not produce anything that they assign any value to. It's interesting to compare the milieu of the traditional high school with a technical high school. We have a couple of these in my area of Maine. The local, traditional high schools are good ones, but like most public high schools, they are rich stews of the talented, the disinterested, the unteachable, the incorrigible, and serious high-achieving kids who would work under any circumstances, like East Germans under communism. But the tech schools are wonders to behold. Offering courses of study in such things as welding, electricity, computers, culinary arts, carpentry, and auto mechanics, the students who attend these schools have, by and large, retained the enthusiasm of kindergartners. Their work is overseen by experts in the respective fields, who guide them through various projects. As they proceed, they witness the gradual creation of some product of their hands. When they were five, it was a potholder; but now it is a rebuilt engine or a well-wired circuit. They are able to step back, wipe their hands, and say, "I did this." In a traditional high school, there are only pale renditions of such events: they come in the form of a paper that bears a letter grade and perhaps a few words from the teacher. For many students, this is not enough to give them any sense that what they are doing is useful.

Last point. Whereas it's self-evident to little kids that they are doing something important, high schoolers are wise to this game.

This is why so many of them believe that school is something they can get along without. Reinforcing this is the perception that we live in an age of easy money. A high school junior watches as his drop-out buddy picks up a construction job and takes home a thousand dollars a week. Another goes to work in the mill and makes equivalent—or better—pay. For a sixteen-year-old, these are riches beyond the dreams of avarice. How can he sit still and listen to a lecture on the shortcomings of the Articles of Confederation when the streets beyond the school are paved with gold?

At the college level, I teach a lot of so-called non-traditional students—those who either did not glide automatically on to college after graduating from high school, or attempted college early on, didn't do well, and have returned, years later, for a second (and usually more successful) shot at it. In these students I feel that I have the best of both worlds: I garner enough child-like enthusiasm from them to make the going worthwhile, and I also observe the sense of purpose and willingness to grapple with books that one sees in the more serious high school students.

The key is this: students are engaged when they think something is at stake. In the elementary schools, fun is at stake. If a kid doesn't do his work, or misbehaves, he forfeits a recess or gets sent to the principal's office. In college, two important things are at stake—money and success. A lot of students are in college precisely because they don't want to work in construction, they don't want to work in the mill. They want something that they dimly define as being "better." That's the promise of college. That's what's at stake.

This leaves us with high school. The *parents* of high schoolers know what is at stake: a diploma and all the doors it will open, all the jobs and colleges it will make possible. But teens are fatalistic about such things. Prodded by hormonal pitchforks, they are marinating in a culture that dictates *Pleasure. Money. Here. Now.* Even for those kids who are not on the verge of dropping out, this message whispers, and it whispers at an age when they are most susceptible to it.

Compared with high school, teaching college is a breeze. By the time a person gets to college—especially if that person is an older student—all the reasons for not being in school have been dealt with and disposed of. I lecture and my students listen, even if they don't always pay attention. I give an assignment and they go off to their computers to work on it.

But as I said in the beginning, there are always "times" when my expectations are not being met, when my college students have lost the "spark" and become as intractable as high schoolers who are distracted by the world without, don't see themselves producing anything worthwhile, and wonder whether they wouldn't be better off simply finding a job. That's when I head for the elementary schools, down to that sea of waving hands and eager faces, to remind myself that "teacher" is one of the most beautiful words in the language. ⚘

⚘ ⚘ ⚘ ⚘ ⚘ ⚘ ⚘ ⚘ ⚘ ⚘ ⚘ ⚘ ⚘ ⚘ ⚘ ⚘ ⚘

beautiful dreamers

Somewhere along the line, during my college teaching career, an assumption (or directive) arose in American society that everyone should—must—go to college. The results have been, in a word, mixed. This prescription often yields nothing but misery for people who became convinced by the "everyone in the college boat" campaign that if they did not get a degree they would fail.

I once had a student—Jason (the quintessential male undergraduate student name)—a milk-faced eighteen-year-old who was personable, sociable, and articulate. When his first biology test turned out to be a disaster, I asked him to stop by my office for a chat. He came in, took a seat, and the dam broke.

(I have to admit here, up front, that I hate it when my students cry. I never know what to do. I recall a young woman who stood face-to-face with me in my office. She suddenly burst into tears and I could sense, from her body language, that she wanted me to hug her. I didn't, and she wrapped her arms about herself, administering the embrace that she must have sensed would not be coming from me.)

Jason told me he was desperately unhappy in school. "Then why are you here?" I asked him. He sniffled and shrugged. "My father told me I had to go to college."

There ensued a brief but heartfelt conversation during which I posed the questions, "Is there anything you do well? Anything that you love?"

Jason wiped his nose on his sleeve and then smiled. "I like to work in the garden," he said. "I like to plant things."

I sat back in my chair and gave him the one piece of unsolicited advice I felt he needed: "Then get out of here and go work for a landscaper."

Jason actually followed my advice. I didn't hear from him for three years. Then, one day, a postcard arrived. It bore a photograph of a magnificent magnolia tree in full bloom, with Jason standing in the foreground. On the reverse he had written: "I have my own business now. I'm happy. Thank you."

Jason was only one of many students I've had who were treading water in the hope that somehow, miraculously, their toes would finally touch bottom and college would suddenly make sense to them. He was occupying a desk for the worst possible reason: the fear of failure if he didn't pursue a degree. As it turned out — before Jason got religion and indulged his passion for petunias — his was a classic case of someone letting college interfere with his education.

There are, at this writing, over four thousand colleges and universities in the United States. It is overkill. Americans are, by and large, particularly ill suited for hunching over books, parsing sentences for their inner meanings, and writing endless dissertations purporting to have identified Emily Dickinson's boyfriend.

Lest I be criticized for a radically bad thought, I'd like to point out that I am, in fact, simply echoing an idea that was first put forward by Alexis de Tocqueville, the peripatetic Frenchman who, in 1831, toured the United States and produced a mammoth report (*Democracy in America*) on our form of government, our institutions, dispositions, and habits. It was de Tocqueville who had it right in the first place. He discerned that the multitudes in America are disposed to utilize knowledge for practical ends, for the vast work of nation-building, while knowledge for the sake of knowledge belongs to the few with what he called a "disinterested passion" for the pursuit of truth. Colleges and universities were meant to house these latter-day academic saints, and for a long time did just that. Today, however, the quest for students at any cost has resulted in success for many but an ungratifying (at best) experience for a significant contingent of others, who while away their four years (or more) of purgatory while dreaming of the places they'd rather be and the things they would rather be doing.

We Americans are, by tradition and inclination, an inventive people. We are an ambitious people. And we are technologically savvy to a dizzying degree as evidenced by the panoply of electronic devices in steady bloom. But none of this requires a college education. After all, one does not attend college in order to become inventive, ambitious, or tech savvy. Those things are part genetic and part imprinted at an early age by the primary inspirational fuel of our culture — the media — with its incessant message to buy, buy, buy, and only the latest, latest, latest (and most expensive).

Nevertheless, semester upon semester, peppered about my classes, are students who idle their time away in a vale of tears, taking up desk space for no other reason than that they were told — by parents or high school guidance counselors or advertising — that if they want to succeed they must attend college. And there they sit, and brood, and . . . fail.

When I say "fail," I don't mean that students who have been

hounded into college despite themselves cannot get good grades. Many of them do. But many fail *themselves* because they have bought into the conventional wisdom that a happy plumber or skilled mason is inferior, or less preferable, to a miserable and mediocre accountant (who, nevertheless, has his diploma neatly framed in his office to vouch for the fact that he took a four-year nap and awoke with a profession that gives him little pleasure and leaves him wishing he were somewhere else).

The thing is, everyone is good at something, or harbors some sort of aptitude. But every such pilot light of ability is not fanned by books and by staring, apoplectically, at a professor as he sketches out *verkakte* theories on the blackboard about Balkan economic systems. We (parents, teachers, guidance counselors) must suppress our misguided desires to mire every kid, no matter their intellectual make-ups or personal preferences, unhappily at a university when someone else could be there who really wants to be.

Such was the case with another male student of mine named Brian. Like Jason, he was bright and personable (except for the intriguing curtain of chestnut hair that he spent much of his time sweeping from his face with aggressive jerks of his head). He was a farm boy with a good work ethic, willing to plow through personal doubt and discontent, achieving A after A on his biology tests.

Then, one day, he showed up in my office with a piece of pastry on a plate. "I made this for you," he said in his clipped, self-effacing way. I tasted and—*Mama mia!*—ambrosia. "Where," I asked him as I brushed the tears from my eyes—"did you learn to bake like this?"

Brian told me that, since he was little, he had loved making desserts. He referred to it as a hobby. I told him that, with such a talent, he could easily hang his shingle wherever he wanted, sending money home to his family and attributing his success to the encouragement of a caring biology professor. "Why are you in college?" I asked him.

He shrugged. "I have no idea," he told me, as if the question had never occurred to him.

I cited his superb biology grades and asked if he'd consider a science major. Brian was flatly honest. "No," he said. "I can't stand science."

"Then what do you want to study?" I asked (as I licked the almond butter from in between two ever-so-delicate sheaths of filo dough).

"No idea."

I thought for only a moment before pronouncing my judgment. "Brian," I said. "Go to cooking school."

He did. And he became a pastry chef in a restaurant in Manhattan, making more money at the outset than I could expect to make by the end of my teaching career. But all of this is tangential, perhaps irrelevant, to the most important fact: Brian had become happy.

There were others:

The young woman who had indentured herself to a biology degree, trying to beat the coursework into her brain like a medieval monk with a flagrum, all the while fantasizing about teaching English in Africa.

The student who had "math anxiety" but was majoring in business because his family had told him—since toddlerhood—that he would be heir to his father's CPA firm. In his spare time he had taught himself German and French and had moved on to Polish. "I wish," he once confided to me, "that I could learn them all."

The young man who spent most of his time in my class staring out the window at the jets as they took off and landed at Bangor International Airport. When I caught him by the arm one day and remarked that he seemed to have his head in the clouds, he smiled and nodded. (He later abandoned his program in psychology to become a pilot.)

The thing is, I identify with all of these students—my beautiful dreamers—in a powerful way. In fact, I've often thought that

if, years ago, someone had given me the advice I so readily dispense today, I would never have attended college at all.

Even in Sacred Heart Elementary School, back in the 1960s, the capricious fury of my sixth-grade nun, Sister Jude, was not enough to discourage me from staring out at the pigeons on the third-story ledge of the apartment building on the other side of Jackson Avenue. How many birds, I wondered, could fit there before one was forced to fly away?

And in my Catholic high school, while Brother William was teaching us how to factor a quadratic equation, I was drawing staff lines and random arrangements of musical notes on pieces of scrap paper, wondering what it would all sound like on my clarinet when I got home.

College was not much of an improvement. In genetics, my most challenging course, I tried my hand at art during those long, involved lectures, by doodling caricatures of my professors on the inside covers of my notebooks.

My mind, in short, has always been elsewhere. How I wound up in biology I'll never know. I feel that my brain is like one of those little, cheapjack, plastic-encased toys, the ones with the BB that rolls around, looking for a hole to fall into. My BB simply fell into the science hole. But it could just as easily have fallen into the foreign language hole, or the carpentry hole, or the music hole. (If I were a student today, I would certainly be diagnosed with some disability or other, prodded by well-meaning technicians intent on maintaining my trajectory toward college.)

And so, duly experienced and sensitized, I persist in identifying the dreamers among my students. I remind myself that many great ideas have revealed themselves to the wandering, rather than the focused, mind. I think of the physicist Leo Szilard, who got the idea for the nuclear chain reaction while waiting for a streetlight to change. Or Einstein, whose voyage toward understanding relativity commenced when he asked himself how the world would look if he could hitch a ride on a beam of light. And what literate person is not familiar with the ancient Greek mathematician Archimedes, who, upon submerging himself into a bathtub and watching the resulting displacement of water, ran through the streets shouting "Eureka!" because he had discovered a means of calculating the volume of solids?

None of my dreamers—those students who had no business being in college—have yet become famous (so far as I know). But almost all the ones who have heeded the better angels of their inclinations and left school for their fields of dreams have become happy.

What a wonderful thing to be. ⚘

the hoary head is a crown of glory

It was the first day of the new semester. I was introducing the course material to the fifteen students in my marine biology class when I noticed her standing on the threshold, her books clutched to her breast like a nervous schoolgirl. Only this student was squat and gray-haired. "Can I help you?" I paused to ask.

The woman glanced about, birdlike, at all the young faces that had turned to her. "I know this class is full," she said, "but I was just wondering if I could sit in."

"Please do," I said, and I watched as she limped into the room and nestled herself among the teens and twenty-somethings.

I normally dedicate the first marine bio class meeting to a survey of my students' native knowledge, to see what they bring to the course. I ask about the difference between a sea and an ocean, what makes a sponge an animal even though it looks like a plant, what evidence we have that whales once walked on land, and even the grammatical difference between the statements,

"Look at all those fish" vs. "Look at all those fishes." (Answer: "those *fish*" refers to members of the same species.)

As usual, I was met with mostly quizzical looks as I plied these waters. But Natalie — the older woman who had requested a box seat — had her hand up at every turn, volunteering answers with the alacrity of a game show contestant. When the class was over and the other students had ambled out (perhaps wondering what they had gotten themselves into), Natalie came up to me, bright and confident, and said, "I'm so sorry this class is full. I'd love to take it."

"Listen," I told her. "You stay and I'll drop the other fifteen students. I don't want to lose you." I added her to the course.

Natalie was in her seventies. She turned out to be as vital and dedicated a student as her debut had augured. She commuted fifty miles each way to get herself and her bad hip to school — often in horrendous Maine winter weather — and never missed a class. She was engaged, enthusiastic, and hard working. Beyond this, she was so contact-friendly and helpful with my younger students that they came to be drawn to her. In Natalie I had more than a good student; I had a role model for the others.

Natalie belonged to a category of students labeled "non-traditional" by institutions of higher learning, meaning they have not followed the customary route of graduating from high school and then automatically plopping into college. They are, as a result, older and, in one way or another, more experienced. In the main, they tend to be more cooperative and organized as well, because cooperation and organization are skills that have helped them build families and succeed in jobs. As a result, they are very rewarding to teach.

Of course, not all older students do well. I have had some who were poorly suited for college, but not because of their age. They were simply not college students, in the same ways that any person, including a recent high school grad, might not be: lack of curiosity, poor or non-existent study habits, aversion to books, laziness. But they have an interesting advantage over their traditional-age cohorts. It lies in the length and depth of their life's path. After having worked at a job, raised a family, and met any number of personal and professional challenges, they have a fairly expansive worldview. While a return to school may at first be intimidating, they tend to succeed because they are taking the trouble to wedge their studies into an already full and multifaceted life. In other words, those who make it do so because they make a commitment to, and because there are very real time pressures involved.

For the traditional-age students, on the other hand, school is almost all they've ever known. In a way, this puts them at a disadvantage, because college can seem like little more than a continuation of high school, lacking the sense of "newness" that often drives curiosity and achievement. I have had many excellent young, traditional-age students who do superbly because they are bright and hard working and are in the habit of getting good grades. But for those who don't succeed, it's often because they take school for granted, and their approach, as a result, is relaxed to the point where they fall behind and finally fall out.

During one laboratory session when Natalie was my student, I distributed a variety of mollusk shells and asked everyone to write descriptive glosses that we would later use to construct a classification key. While many of the younger students were daunted and frustrated by the assignment, Natalie went about it with the wide-eyed enthusiasm of a first-grader, handling the shells and remarking on their beauty. And then, in the course of student chatter, a young woman asked Natalie what her first job had been. "Well," she said, "I was a gunnery instructor in World War II." A gunnery instructor! From a legendary war. (Most of the other students had been born after Vietnam.) The rest of the class fell silent. While they were fretting over the clam shells, Natalie looked at the assignment as simply something new to be learned in a lifetime filled with interesting chapters. Her sense of perspective and her energetic approach earned her the highest grades in the class.

There have been others, of course. The forty-year-old mother of three who, instead of doing the five required lab assignments, completed thirteen and then somehow managed to go to sea on an oceanographic expedition. The twenty-six-year-old Penobscot Indian who completed my course in stellar fashion and went on to complete his Ph.D. The thirty-year-old man who took my marine biology course and, duly inspired, became a deep-sea ("hard-hat") diver. These are real, palpable achievements, made by people who were already well along in life. Their accomplishments are more remarkable when one considers that, for many of them, their earlier schooling augured anything but success. These latter are the most interesting and, for me, gratifying cases: those successful non-traditional students who, through their own undoing or because of forces beyond their control, had had disastrous experiences in high school but now were excelling in college.

Here I must admit to a serious bias: through personal experience and cool observation, I have come to believe that high school is often little more than a holding pen for kids suffering from testosterone and estrogen poisoning. For the "good" boys and girls — those obedient sons and daughters who truly are the academic apples of their parents' eyes — it works well enough, and provides a smooth path toward adulthood; but for many, many others, both teachers and parents are hard-pressed to give these young people a reason why they should be in school. The best rationale I can come up with is that, in these cases, the high school is a kind of minimum security facility designed to protect society-at-large until these anti-students can be safely re-released into the community.

I wasn't one of those kids. But I knew many who were. In my own New Jersey high school, I still remember the teachers chasing Anthony Carlucci through the hallways as he slammed lockers and tore posters from the walls while belting out a respectable rendition of "Helter Skelter." Anthony wanted out, that's all. He didn't have ADHD or ADD or any other acronym that didn't exist at the time. He just needed to fly, but instead was all but shackled to his desk, where he whiled away his four years plotting mischief. Needless to say, he didn't go on to college. Instead, he took his C-minuses and D's and F's and hit the highway, à la Jack Kerouac. The tidbits of intel that I received after the fact indicated that he had worked as a motorcycle mechanic, spent time in prison in the south, became a cashier, blew an engine through the hood of his GTO while doing 135 on I-95, and then, after more jail time, entered a period of quiescence. Finally, I received word that Anthony, in his thirties, had completed college with a bachelor's degree in elementary education (!). Then he got his master's, then a certificate of advanced study that enabled him to obtain a principalship. He earned a reputation for being strict but fair.

I would not have liked to teach a sixteen-year-old Anthony Carlucci. Hell, most of the time I didn't even like being his friend (although there was a little something deep inside the tractable, obedient, studious me that envied his wild ways). But I would have enjoyed — to the hilt — having him in college as one of my students at a more settled period of his life, where he would display cooperation and hard work and I would be mindful of the tumultuous road he had traveled to get to a point where learning was at least possible.

On another note — a vain one — there is another fundamental difference between older, non-traditional students and their teenage classmates: they are aware of me. Where teenagers tend to be self-absorbed to the point of obliviousness, the older students really know I'm there. They talk to me, answer my questions, and laugh at my jokes. Sometimes they bring me cake. I like it.

As for Natalie, at the end of the course I was sad to see her go, but happy that her experience in my class had been a rich one. Despite her bad hip, she insisted on hobbling along on field trips. Her hearing was not what it used to be, so she sat right up front and strained to gather my lectures. At the end of the course, when Natalie came at me with a grandmotherly kiss on the cheek, I accepted gracefully.

I have kept track of her over the years. She lives in a little house on the coast of Maine. She paid twelve thousand dollars for it several decades ago — at a time when it was possible for a person of modest means to own land on the coast of Maine — and recently made the final payment on her thirty-year mortgage. Her plans? To spend her life savings to travel to New Zealand to observe the marine life there. I take some ownership in that. For my part, I make a point of stopping in to see Natalie whenever I am down her way. I usually bring her a little something: a bag of oranges or a loaf of fresh bread. Then we sit and chat.

I read somewhere that the average age of undergraduate students is now twenty-seven and rising. If this is true, then my best years of teaching may yet be ahead of me. ⚘

following the dead (or, why attendance matters)

Invariably, it is the question that punctuates my first lecture of the semester. Like a noxious bubble of methane rising — inexorably — through that initial swamp of student anxiety as they try to size up both me and my biology course, it voices itself with all the tension and anticipation of Oliver Twist requesting that momentous second helping of gruel.

"Does attendance count?"

What seems on the surface like a trivial query is actually larded with gravity. When that tremulous student finds the courage to ask this question — as if representing the hopes and aspirations of the entire class — I am always thrown into a mental mire of uncertainty. And my answers, I'm sure, have never been satisfactory.

Attendance. Shouldn't the task of making a daily head count be the purview of the elementary and high schools, where the specter of *liability* hovers over the teachers and administrators should they lose track of a child? College is supposed to be different. Our students are, legally at least, adults. Shouldn't they be responsible for managing their own time? If they're paying for a course, isn't it up to them to decide whether to attend or not?

These are, for the moment, rhetorical questions and do not necessarily represent my personal conclusions. I have, over the years, come to realize that the issue of attendance is not simple.

When I began my college teaching career, I was all for free will. While other professors ran their classes with quasi-military precision and expectations (students confined to their desks, scribbling in their notebooks), my classroom operated more like a buffet. Students came and went with all the capriciousness of leaves caught up in an autumn wind. Sometimes they would arrive halfway through the class, walking right in front of me while I lectured, and then, once seated, ask, "Can you tell me what you've been talking about?"

An erstwhile colleague of mine once noted the Summer of Woodstock atmosphere of my classroom. Jack was a tall, phlegmatic, rather cut-and-dried professor of biology who spent as little time as possible on campus. Where the offices of most science professors resembled moving-in day at the thrift shop, Jack's space was as clean and austere as a monk's cell. His only nod to acquisitiveness was a gull's wing hanging from a string over his desk, the perhaps unintended message being, "See? I too can collect, but there are limits."

Jack was a veteran teacher whose afterburners of enthusiasm had long since sputtered out, and his solution to student attendance, like his approach to everything else, was black and white. When the hour struck for his class to begin, he simply locked the door. Should a student not get the message and venture to knock, Jack would ignore the interruption. Should the student be insistent and continue knocking, Jack would eventually go over to the door, open it a crack, and remark, "Why don't you, er, take a walk?" And that would be that.

I had to admit to a grudging respect for the peace Jack had made with his soul on this issue. But I just wasn't built for such a two-dimensional existence. Whenever I considered reading my students the riot act over attendance and punctuality, my blood ran, well, not cold, but cool. I didn't want attendance to be dismissed by my students as unimportant, but neither did I want it to become an obsession for me. My class did, at times, resemble a talk show on which students made cameo appearances, but it always seemed more important to go on with the material than take a break to deliver a lecture on classroom etiquette.

Which is where Mark comes in. Mark was a Deadhead, a follower of the Grateful Dead while Jerry Garcia was still very much alive and kicking. I can still see Mark sitting—on occasion—in my introductory biology course. With his shag haircut, flannel shirt, wooly vest, and jeans torn at the knees, he was too young to have known hippie culture, but he did his best to echo it.

I never really understood why Mark was taking biology, and I don't think he did either. I think his lack of a raison d'être for science made it all the easier for him to disappear from time to time. Now and then I would arrive in class and find, without warning, a note plastered to his desktop: FOLLOWING THE DEAD.

What this meant, of course, was that he was on the road again, going where the Grateful Dead went. Mark, a pauper who lived in a slum of an apartment with a nest of his fellow-student paupers, supported his junkets by selling tie-dyed Grateful Dead T-shirts to the groupies at the concerts. And then, after his hiatus, and without warning, he would reappear in class, leaning back in his desk with his hands knotted behind his head. The look on his face bespoke one word: contentment.

Mark came and went like the tides, while his grades meandered along like a streamlet that carried only seasonal moisture and was constantly on the brink of drying up. I flirted with the idea of giving him an either/or proposition: Either you come to class or drop the course. But I could never bring myself to draw such a line. Truth to tell, I harbored a genuine warmth for Mark. Not so much because he was a nice person (which he was), but because, without ever uttering a biological term or stubbing a mental toe on an insight, he somehow made my class interesting. In short, I couldn't imagine Mark's not being part of that class, however spotty his attendance. When he was there, he was funny and exuded a sense of well-being that was contagious and seemed to put heart into the other students; when he wasn't there, all of us envisioned his T-shirt-hawking antics while following the Dead, and we all anticipated his return with smiles on our faces.

Still, I was conflicted about the general philosophy of class attendance. Eventually, my thoughts roamed to the accomplishments of Rudolf Virchow, a nineteenth-century Prussian who was arguably the most famous European physician of his time.

Virchow was a fascinating figure. Diligent, brilliant, insatiably curious, and a believer in life-long learning, he had a passion for histology (the study of tissues), developed the first truly scientific protocol for autopsies, and saved countless lives as a result of his insistence on preventive medicine to thwart disease before it got a foothold in the body. An interesting sidelight of Virchow's career, and a tribute to his reputation throughout Europe, is that during one of their world tours, the original Siamese twins, Chang and Eng, consulted Virchow about the possibility of severing the ligament that joined them at the chest. But, as Mark Twain wrote in his classic satirical essay on the twins, ". . . they were inseparable companions," and Virchow—while the world watched and waited with bated breath—finally pronounced that he didn't dare make such an attempt, as he didn't know whether the ligament contained any vital material. (X-rays were still some forty years in the future.)

Above and beyond the mechanics of his practical achievements, Virchow is notable for the formulation of an overarching statement about the nature and importance of cells. As preamble — and to provide a certain degree of drama — it is important to say something about the history of cell biology.

Before the seventeenth century, no one had ever seen a cell. More fundamentally, no one even suspected that such things as cells existed. Enter the Englishman Robert Hooke.

Hooke was, at root, a brilliant inventor who favored experiment over theory. One day — the exact date is unknown — he was observing specimens with his microscope. He came to a piece of cork, which is eminently sliceable. He took a shaving with his straight razor, thin enough for light to pass through. When he placed the cork on his microscope and illuminated it — choir of angels! blare of trumpets! — he made history. What he saw were tiny, empty, thin-walled chambers. He immediately dubbed them cells, as they reminded him of the cells that monks slept in. In 1665 he published the first-ever description of a cell in his masterpiece, the *Micrographia*, the first important work on microscopy.

Two hundred years passed between Hooke's discovery in the mid-seventeenth century and Virchow's heyday in the mid-nineteenth century. In the interim, other researchers had occupied themselves in mighty fashion with studying the diversity of cells, as well as (within the limits of the chemistry and instrumentation of the times) their function. But no one had, as yet, come up with an all-encompassing statement about the core significance of cells to all living things. This is exactly what Virchow did. He is credited with what is known as the "Cell Theory." Here it is, paraphrased: "All living things are made up of self-reproducing units called cells." (Two earlier biologists, Matthias Schleiden and Theodor Schwann, had also suggested a cell theory, but they erred when they stated that new cells formed in a manner similar to crystals. It was Virchow who recognized that all cells come from the division of other cells.)

Like many groundbreaking concepts in science, this one is direct, concise, and elegant. Virchow wasn't saying that cork is made of cells and so are dogs. He didn't say that plants but not animals are made of cells. He said *all* living things are made of cells. If science is the search for theories that summarize, bind, and show interconnections, then Virchow had earned his pay with his great idea.

As I recall, Mark the Deadhead wasn't in class when we discussed the cell theory. But it was precisely his absence on that particular day that offered me, at long last, some insight regarding class attendance. As I glanced from the words on the blackboard ("Cell Theory") to Mark's empty desk, it became clear to me, perhaps with the same force with which the term "cell" had revealed itself to Hooke when he studied that sliver of cork, why Mark—and everyone else—needed to be there.

Yes, students are free agents. Yes, they are paying for the course. Yes, they are adults. *Granted. Given. Understood.* But a class is, in the words of my son's public school, a community of learners. A partnership between teacher and students. If a course is run well, and is interesting, then it represents nothing less than a narrative. In this light, whenever someone is absent, the plot suffers because a character, for no apparent reason, has disappeared. In short, the personality of the community is compromised, because a valuable (or potentially valuable) voice is missing, as if it had been suddenly silenced. This led me, in the spirit of Virchow, to create a grand Attendance Theory. Here it is: "All classes are communities of learners, and each voice is valuable and essential to the course narrative. When you are absent you compromise the narrative's plot. Therefore, attendance is important and expected. Unexcused absences may affect your grade."

Perhaps not enough pedagogical fire and brimstone for the taste of my colleague Jack, but I now felt better about things.

As for Mark, he got through biology, but barely. After that, I never saw him again. But I do think of him from time to time. ⚹

what i say and what they hear

"I have a sin of fear," wrote the seventeenth-century English poet John Donne regarding his unsteady faith in God. I also have a sin of fear, but it is a far more mundane one: that I will see the contents of one of my student's notebooks.

As I stand before my class, lecturing, my students look like court stenographers, their pens wagging without letup as they try to get down on paper every word that I utter, as if I were a prophet and they were creating a historical record for future generations of the faithful.

It's a deceptive image. Even though it *looks* as if they are transcribing my lecture verbatim, what winds up in their notebooks is anything but. I know this from grim experience.

It's like this. Every so often, once my students have vacated the classroom, I spot a notebook that has been left behind. *Damn*, I think. *Now I have to pick it up.* My hope is that there will be a name on the cover, which means I won't have to open it to look for one. But more often than not there is no identifier, and I must crack the notebook to seek out some i.d. In the course of my search I can't help but notice their biology notes, as well as ancillary scribblings. It is like spotting the Rubber Man at the circus. I simply can't look away.

These books of revelations contain information that falls broadly into three categories of the remarkable. Let me enumerate them.

The first category comprises unsolicited editorial comments —running critiques of my lectures. For example, during the ecology section of my general biology course, I detail how eating lower on the food chain makes more food available for everyone. "It takes one hundred pounds of grain to make ten pounds of beef," I narrate as I show the class an overhead transparency of a lump of ground beef next to a sack of feed. "Do you think you could feed more people with ten pounds of beef or a hundred pounds of grain?" Heads nod and pens dance. But after one such lecture I found a notebook on the seat of a desk. Heaving a sigh, I approached it with cautious abandon. My heart sank when I saw its blank cover. I picked it up and paged through. Still no name, but in the margin of the ecology lecture notes was the gloss, "Save cows! Eat a vegetarian!"

Other interesting asides I've collected over the years are:

"Darwin is stuped! [sic]"
"I just don't understand this."
"Why is he teaching us chemistry? I though this was biology."
"How old is Klose?"

The second category is the caricature, generally flattering. In the forgotten notebook of one young woman — apparently with time on her hands — was a detailed sketch of me with a big bobble head and itty-bitty body, along with the comment, "Nice sweater." On another occasion a student had sketched three faculty members, including me, and labeled us, in turn, "good," "bad" and "ugly." (With craven disregard for the feelings of the other two, I feel compelled to report that I was the one labeled "good.")

Both of the above categories provide me with modest interest, but the category that truly disconcerts me is the one that records comments I know I never made. For better or worse, these are the types of notes that best tell me whether or not I am getting the information across.

Evolution is a major tar pit of misapprehensions. I take great pains to emphasize, for example, that Darwin never used his theory of natural selection to explain how life on earth originated. He only sought to describe how species have physically changed in concord with an ever-changing environment. But this does not stop some students from making wild statements in their notes, one of the preeminent being, "Darwin said it was natural selection instead of God that created the earth. This is how humans came to be."

What does one do when one stumbles upon such a comment? (My reaction is almost as strong as it would be if I had found that a student had written, "There is a bomb in this building.") I normally have a hands-off policy toward my students' notebooks. The reason I don't want to see what their notes look like is that I don't want to struggle with the temptation to make corrections or appear to be invading a student's privacy. But sometimes I take the student aside, describe how I happened to see a misstatement in his or her notebook, and set things straight as expediently and gently as I can.

Sometimes the lecture material is not as conceptual as evolution, just crudely factual. "Atoms have protons, neutrons, and electrons." "Genes are made of DNA." "Robert Hooke coined the term 'cell.'" Still, there are times when even these compact fragments undergo some sort of transmutation during the transit between my lips and my students' notebooks. Take the strange and recurring case of Anton van Leeuwenhoek and his association with the microscope.

Leeuwenhoek was a seventeenth-century Dutch draper who had little formal education. For the same unknown reason that probably drives all geniuses, he developed a passion for something very specific — in his case, lenses — and became an expert grinder of very small versions of these gems. He mounted his lenses in hand-held frames to create simple microscopes that were really little more than very fine magnifying glasses.

Now, it's important to note here that the microscope was invented — also in the Netherlands — a hundred years before Leeuwenhoek's time by a man named Janssen. But despite the availability of such a powerful tool, no one had ever observed microscopic life with it. In other words, the microscope, up until Leeuwenhoek, was more of a novelty than a scientific instrument. As fate would have it, it was the marginally educated Leeuwenhoek who first applied the microscope to the invisible living world and changed science in a truly monumental way.

It was like this. One day, Leeuwenhoek was picking his teeth. He noticed some tartar on the toothpick and wondered, in his inimitable childlike manner, what it might look like under the microscope. So he mixed it with a little water and observed. What he saw astounded him: minuscule wiggling forms that he called "little beasties" (now known to have been bacteria). Thus Leeuwenhoek became the first human to view microscopic life, which earned him the moniker, "Father of Microbiology."

I tell this story to my students in great detail, but for some reason the connection *Leeuwenhoek — microscope* (rather than *Leeuwenhoek — microscopic life*) makes the primary impact, and both their tests and "found" notebooks contain this misinformation: "Leeuwenhoek invented the microscope." I have been frustratingly unable to disabuse them of this false idea. My last recourse has been to make them recite the following mantra, over and over, during our section on cell biology: "Leeuwenhoek did not invent the microscope. Leeuwenhoek did not invent the microscope. Leeuwenhoek . . ."

Just when I seemed to be making some headway in giving both Leeuwenhoek and Janssen their due, I came upon a forgotten notebook after one of my lectures. No name on the cover. So I opened it, and there, nestled among the last pages of notes was, "Leeuwenhoek invented the microscope."

Once again, to alert the student or not? I should have simply closed the thing and given it back to its owner; but instead I seized my pen and, under the student's incorrect information, scribbled, "He did not." The next day, I returned the notebook.

A period of calm ensued, during which we went on to the next topic. A couple of days later, though, that student held up a book in class. It was a newly published biography of the Austrian monk Gregor Mendel who, in the nineteenth century, had formulated the basic laws of heredity. "It says here," began my eager student — ruefully — "that Leeuwenhoek invented the microscope."

Stunned silence. The entire class turned to me, their faces full of appeal. "Give me the book," I said, and the student handed it over. I stood before the class and read the passage to myself. There it was, in black and white, "Anton van Leeuwenhoek . . . created the world's first microscope." I glanced up at the student who had given me the book, and he looked smug, as if to say, "So what do you think of *that*, Mr. College Professor?"

"Well," I said, unmoved by what he considered his coup, "this author is mistaken."

"But it's in the book!" exclaimed my nemesis.

Our confrontation ended in a draw, with neither of us willing to give ground. Of course, I was confident in my knowledge of the facts, but that didn't stop this student from stirring up the class with his carved-in-stone evidence that I was wrong about a landmark event in the history of biology, and there ensued a melee of cross-examination of several other of the tenets of biology I had presented. I soon felt like a politician losing the support of his constituency.

I had only one recourse. After my lecture I went to the nearest computer and found the website of the author of that book. I diplomatically informed her that Leeuwenhoek had not invented the microscope, and that it was a common misconception that he had.

The next day the author sent me a gracious reply, acknowledging the mistake and pledging to rectify it in subsequent editions of her book, if any.

I printed out her e-mail and read it to my class, like a proclamation. They took my word that the document was authentic, and peace was restored among my students, including the one who had raised the fuss in the first place.

What all of this points up is that note-taking is exactly that: notes, or glosses, reflecting the essence of what a professor is saying during the course of what might be a long-winded narration. In actuality, though, very, very few students take notes. Almost all of them attempt to transcribe, word-for-word, what the professor is saying; hence the insistent and repetitive questions and directives: "Could you say that again?" "Slow down, I didn't get it all." "Can you spell that?"

Is this a major problem? Well, yes it is. If a student is trying to write down everything the professor is saying, then there is absolutely no time to *think* about whether what they are hearing is meaningful or not. The result is often misinformation ("Leeuwenhoek invented the microscope"), which I discover only when I get a peek inside a forgotten notebook, or, more irrevocably and tragically, when a test is given.

What about those students who feel they can't keep up because they can't write fast enough? Well, this is where their unsolicited margin comments and caricatures come in.

Whether a student belongs to the cohort that is trying to write everything down or the one that quits and doodles because it can't, both would benefit from the same solution: requiring all entering freshmen to take a one-credit course in note-taking. An hour a week is all it would require to teach them to listen for key words and to write meaningful fragments rather than paragraphs. If they learn to be skillful at this, all they would need to do would be to connect the dots, as it were, to re-create a narrative whole that tells them everything they need to know.

Of course, this would also mean the end of the era of the "found" notebook and its attendant wonders. ⚹

the impossible dream

I went to an all-boys prep school, where the assumption was that all its graduates would go on to college. There was no vocational or technical track. When I entered as a fourteen-year-old freshman in 1968 (two years before the Beatles broke up, alas), the teachers wasted no time in orienting us to our objective: in fewer than fifteen hundred days we would be shoving off for a college or university, where we would excel, making our family, friends, and alma mater proud, and then we would go on to fulfilling and prosperous careers, which would enable us to remit checks to the school's alumni association as gestures of gratitude for the superb secondary education we had received.

By senior year I was equivocal about going to college, but there was that presumption of its being the next logical step; and besides, all my friends were doing it. Like them, I was superbly prepared for higher education: four years of math, four of Spanish, four of English, four of history, plus biology, chemistry, and physics. I applied to five colleges and was accepted by all of them.

I enrolled as a chemistry major. Then I saw something in the newspaper about chemists and brain cancer, so I moderated my major to biochemistry, feeling I could thereby escape contact with some of the more toxic organic compounds. But then, just as I was poised to leave for college, I changed my major again, to marine biology, when I discovered that the curriculum required a semester's sojourn at the school's marine lab in the Virgin Islands.

I had a rough start in college, perhaps because I presumed it would be easy. So, after a mediocre first semester, I doubled down, putting in twenty hours of study for my chemistry tests and a few hours less for biology, which came easier to me.

Through it all I worked evenings in a funeral home, doing my homework in the casket showroom when business was slow. I pushed myself so hard that I wound up at the doctor's office, where he told me I was suffering from stress. At the tender age of eighteen! But still I pushed on, year after year, and finished with a flourish: a 4.0 GPA my last three semesters.

Now, I tell this story not to extol myself as a model student (I wasn't: I got a D in my first college physics course. I also once fed a Big Mac to an immense sea anemone that lived in one of the bio labs), but rather to describe the experience of someone who was well prepared for college, understood what was involved, was able to improve when his grades flagged, and who availed himself of extra help when he needed it.

So what does one do with the opposite type of student: one who is not prepared for college, does not understand the work, cannot extricate himself from the mire of failing or near-failing grades, and doesn't go for extra help because he doesn't know what questions he wants to ask?

It wasn't long after I began teaching college that I was finally confronted with such a student. I tried every trick, repeatedly spoke to the student to get at the root of the problem, and consulted counselors for their insights. Dustin was a conundrum. What's more, he was a conundrum who had almost no interpersonal skills: rail-thin and gangly, whenever I spoke to him he'd look down at the floor, his large brown eyes laden with a one-two whammy of haplessness and palpable sadness. When he replied, in short bursts of non sequiturs, he'd continue to stare down at the floor. I wanted to take him by the shoulders, give a good shake, and say, "Dustin, look at me." But I didn't. I was afraid I might shake him to pieces.

My school has an open admissions policy. For a college teacher, this is the ultimate double-edged sword. On the one hand, everybody gets a chance to show that he or she can do college-level work, no matter the complications of their life's road. On the other, clearly unprepared and marginally capable students are led to believe that getting a college degree is little more than a matter of marking time. The result of this open door is a crazy quilt of success stories and catastrophes and everything in between. Caught in the middle is the teacher, who is expected to provide a challenging educational experience for all types of students in the same classroom.

Dustin was one of the catastrophes. But there was more at work than just poor academic aptitude. It was that rigid mask of sadness, the sputtered speech, the unkempt hair. It was as if somebody had pulled him off the street, stuck a pen and notebook in his hands, and sat him down in a college classroom with one directive: learn.

I didn't say anything to Dustin until he had taken his first test. Why should I have? He was quiet and cooperative, if sociophobic: when I had the students pair up in lab, he made no move to work with anybody else and, no doubt because of his dark demeanor, the other students didn't show an interest in working with him. The most I ventured at those times was the occasional, "Is everything okay?" that elicited only a brisk nod.

His first test was a disaster. Not a D. Not just failing. The grade was irretrievably low: I couldn't even concoct rationales for a few extra points by giving credit for, say, good handwriting or complete sentences. The content was incorrect, as if Dustin hadn't been sitting in my class for three weeks. The ideas were jumbled. He had left blank spaces for some very elementary questions, including a true/false. At last I had a legitimate reason to call him to my office for a chat.

He sat down opposite me, focusing sidelong on the floor tiles, as if expecting a cockroach to scurry out of the woodwork. His straight blond hair, parted down the middle, framed and largely obscured his face, affording only a Zen view of his features. I began my interrogation, using the test as a prop as I held it out between us. "What happened?" I asked, almost offhandedly, as if his grade were no big deal.

His rat-a-tat-tat response: "I don't know. I studied. I understood everything. That's only the first test. I'll do better on the next."

"Do you want extra help?"

Still staring down at the floor tiles, "I don't think I need it. I just have to study more."

I already knew that studying more was not the answer. Dustin seemed oblivious to the material. I pointed out a specific question. "Look here, Dustin," I said, and his eyes shifted to the test I was holding in front of him. "The question reads, 'differentiate between the evolutionary theories of LaMarck and Darwin.' But your answer was about the subdisciplines of biology."

Pause. Then the machine gun response: "Well-it's-something-you-talked-about-so-I-thought-it-was-right."

I firmed my lip. "Dustin, let me ask you something. When I give my lectures, do you understand what I'm talking about?"

"Sometimes."

"But you never ask questions when you don't understand."

No response.

"This isn't the end of the world," I said. "There are four tests and I drop the lowest one. Let's consider this your dropped test, press 'reset,' and look for a better grade on the next one."

Dustin got up and headed for the door. "Okay. Thank you," he said, mechanically, and left.

Three weeks later I gave my students their next test. I watched as Dustin scribbled away with the élan of the confident young scholar. He was the last to finish. "How did it go?" I asked as he handed his paper in.

A fleeting smile crossed his lips. "I did better on this one," he said, and walked away.

I immediately sat down to correct his test. As soon as I began, my heart sank. It was in line with the first. The handwriting was all but illegible — great swooping jumbles of rounded letters. And, once again, many of the answers didn't line up with the questions. There was also too much information, a stream of consciousness of randomized lecture material. It was as if Dustin were throwing everything he had heard in class onto the paper, like a man in a sinking ship, frantically tossing ballast overboard. His grade, once again, was low, beyond the pale. It was clear that Dustin would not pass the course.

I took a few minutes to gather my thoughts and then called the school counselor. I told him that Dustin was not doing well and had no prospect of improving. "It's as if I'm speaking a language he doesn't understand," I said.

I could hear the counselor rummaging through his files. "Let me take a look at his rec . . . Oh, boy."

"You found something?"

"Yeah. His aptitude scores. I've never seen scores this low."

We both paused in silence. Then I ventured onto the counselor's turf. "I sense that there's more to this student than just poor academic skills."

He heaved a sigh. "You're right," he said. "But I can't . . ."

"Don't tell me. Confidentiality."

"Yeah."

That was the end of the conversation. I realized that both Dustin and I were in impossible situations. He couldn't pass biology and I was operating in the dark. The counselor's silence implied that I had no right or need to know anything about Dustin's background — information, perhaps, that could have helped me to help him. I found myself angry with the school for placing this student into a hopelessly frustrating situation. Even in an open admissions institution, I felt that the student must bring something to the table that the instructor can work with, and that it was the duty of the admissions office to confirm that the student had this "something." With Dustin I had next to nothing. I called him back to my office to make what I thought was a fair and generous offer.

Once again he sat there, his eyes cast to the side, his head inclined as if he were listening to distant voices. "Dustin," I said, handing the second test to him. "It didn't go well this time either."

"I don't understand," he said as he turned the pages. "I thought I knew it."

"You're not grasping this material," I said.

"I'll have to study harder."

I shook my head. "You're not understanding me. It's not a matter of crossing a few more t's or making sure that you underline scientific names. You're not grasping the concepts at all and you won't ask for help. It's painful to see this course passing over you like a steamroller."

Dustin glanced at me, and the sight of his eyes, deep and woeful, shook me. "What do you want me to do?" he asked.

"Despite your low grades, I'm willing to offer you a withdraw pass."

"But I can start to do better," he said by way of protest.

I slowly shook my head. "The material is only going to get more complicated as we go on," I told him.

His expression hardened. "You're trying to discourage me," he said.

"I'm giving you a chance to find the door that's open to you," I countered. "This one is clearly closed."

He wouldn't accept the offer. "No," he said. "I'm going to do better."

I couldn't force him to withdraw, so the band played on. As a means of gaining some insight into how he learned, I told Dustin that we would study together. "You have no choice," I said. "You must see me for two hours a week until the next test. To make sure you understand the material."

After Dustin left my office I questioned what I had proposed. Did I believe I could force Dustin to learn? Or worse, was I doing his work for him? But it was my scientific curiosity that got the better of me: I needed to know how he approached the material, what went through his head when he read a word like "lysosome," and why he thought that his irrelevant answers were pertinent to the questions.

To his credit, Dustin showed up session after session. As

much as possible, we scheduled our meetings on the heels of the lectures, so that the material would be fresh in his head. The third section of the course dealt with basic chemistry. I started with a discussion of the elements, how they are logically organized on the periodic table, and the contribution of the great Russian chemist, Dmitri Mendeleev, who formulated the table. Then I moved on to atomic structure and bonding. Working with Dustin was a process of discovery. I'd like to be able to say that I came to understand how he learned; but it was exactly the opposite: I was finally able to see how he didn't learn. Somewhere between my lips and his ears, the information became garbled, as if embedded in static.

"Dustin," I said as we sat side-by-side at my desk. "Take a look at this table of the elements. Tell me anything you can about it. Do you see any patterns?"

"Hmm," he said as he scanned the chemical symbols. "It's not alphabetized."

"No, it's not. What else?"

"A lot of letters."

"What do those letters stand for?"

"Elements?"

And so it went. The periodic table of the elements, to me, is a metaphor for the very idea of science: order, categorization, pattern. Dustin perceived none of this. When I asked for patterns he noted non-patterns. It was as if there were a Teflon interface between him and the material. If I said, "Elements contain atoms and atoms contain protons, neutrons, and electrons," he couldn't get these relationships right, similar to a toddler who can't stack his blocks.

He took the third test. Result: failure. Not as bad as the first two tests, but not enough progress to get him out of the hole. Once again I suggested that he take the offer of a withdraw pass. He said nothing, but that evening I received an e-mail from him. "You're trying to make me hopeless," he wrote, and this stung me. But I had misapprehended my own response, and by the next morning I realized that it wasn't hurt I felt, but sadness. For Dustin. Not only could he not make sense of the course material, but he also could not perceive the human concern I was trying to show him.

He insisted on studying for the final exam on his own. Result: disaster. He failed the course and I never saw him or heard from him again. I don't know where he went.

Did I give up on this student? Or was Dustin ever a student in the first place? Did I do enough for him, or did I try to do too much? We consistently tell our students — in the elementary grades as well as in high school and college — that they can be whatever they choose to be. I think this philosophy serves important political purposes, especially in the lower grades, because one of the jobs of the teacher is to encourage. But in moments of quiet consideration, I'm sure I'm not alone in acknowledging that not every dream is achievable, especially as time goes on and students' abilities and proclivities and limitations come into sharper focus. Whatever Dustin's background may have been, whatever trauma he may have suffered, I believe that college was the wrong place for him. What virtue is there in telling a blind person that he can drive a car?

Despite all of this, I regret that Dustin disappeared so unceremoniously. I don't know what I would have said to him had I seen him one more time. But I would have been very interested in his thoughts, and what he planned to do next. ♠

the death of fiction

I have never understood why students feel obligated to concoct fantastic stories regarding absences, missed tests and assignments, and the inability to meet deadlines. Do they fear my reaction if they were simply to say, "I'm sorry I was absent. Can I give you the assignment today?"

The compulsion to explain one's circumstances is not limited to the classroom. I was in the bank the other day and stood behind a woman speaking to a teller. She asked to withdraw five hundred dollars. That's where I would have stopped; but for some reason she seemed chagrined about this request, lowered her voice, and confided to the teller, "I don't usually take out this much money, but my son is short this month. He has a good job, though, and when he repays me I'll deposit it again."

The teller nodded passively as he counted out the bills, but the customer looked uncomfortable, as if she were doing something unorthodox, like facing the back of a crowded elevator. She conveyed the distinct impression that it was the bank's money she was requesting and that they might be judging her for her lack of self-control.

Likewise, I was once riding the city bus when it stopped to allow an elderly man to get on. He deposited his fare and then sheepishly explained to the driver that he realized this wasn't the bus he usually took and that he would get back on track with his usual bus in the morning.

I think college students are similarly afflicted. What is it about college that brings out the apologist in them? Where do they get their ability to craft such glib narratives? After all, these are people who generally don't read books for pleasure and look upon writing as an artifact from the age of cuneiform. Let me give some examples, moving from the mundane to the sublime.

At the end of the spring semester of biology, I routinely inform my class that I will give the final exam only once and would not come to school during the summer to give make-ups. Any student who missed the final would have to wait until the end of the fall semester and take the test with the next class. Despite this, one student, Matt, made himself conspicuous by being the only absentee. I dutifully recorded an "I" (incomplete) for his grade. Two weeks later he came to my office. "I missed the final," he said.

"Yes," I confirmed. "The class was greatly upset."

Whereupon he commenced his monologue. "You see, I woke up early, because I didn't want to miss the final, because biology is my favorite class. But when I saw that it was raining I rolled over and went back to sleep."

I put my hand on his shoulder. "Matt," I said. "I have to compliment you on your courage. I'd be ashamed to admit that to my teacher."

In Maine, the winter always provides a ready excuse for missed classes or assignments. Such was the case when a student rushed into the classroom fifteen minutes late. "I'm so sorry I don't have my assignment," she said, panting. "I was running out of the house with it, but I was in such a hurry that I dropped it and the man snowblowing my driveway . . ."

". . . sucked it up with the snowblower," I interjected.

The student looked at me, relieved at my understanding. "How did you know?" she asked.

"That's the way I would have ended the story."

One more. A young woman missed a laboratory exercise she needed to keep her grade in the passing range. She eventually showed up a few days later. "You'll never believe what happened," she said.

"You had to withdraw five hundred dollars from the bank because your son can't manage his money?"

She looked at me. "My son is three," she said.

"Go on, then."

"Well, I was rushing to class, driving up the hill in Charleston. You know the hill?"

"Of course."

"Well, at the top of the hill I ran out of gas. I got confused and the car rolled back down. But there was a cop at the bottom of the hill. He gave me a ticket for speeding backwards. I was so upset that I had to go home and lie down."

It had to be true. How could anyone make up such a thing? In fact, I believe all these stories, for the same reason illustrated by the woman at the bank: the deep-seated human need to explain one's circumstances, which students assume are so compelling that embellishment is unnecessary. But there is more to it than this. An excuse can also be seen as a complaint, and complaints serve a self-ennobling purpose. The late social psychologist Sheldon Kopp once wrote that complaining is a way of showing that we can take it. In this light, I presume my students, in divulging the sometimes-intimate complications of their lives, are making this statement: "Despite what has befallen me, and in the very depths of my travails, I want you to know that I fully intend to pass biology."

There was a time, not long ago, when I was impatient with these stories. But then I came to appreciate them as cultural narratives, some of which describe personal challenges ("I can't get out of bed in the morning. Nobody in my family can") or good intentions ("I did the work last night and put it on the kitchen table, but then . . ."). Other tales qualify as heroic epics ("I missed the laboratory session because the road was flooded, so I had to get out of my car and wade through the water while holding my books over my head") and tragedies ("Little did I know that the assignment I was doing was, indeed, the wrong one").

And then there is a category of excuses that forms a complex genre of its own because it is gender-specific, requiring as its base ingredient a unique, recurring character — the helpless boyfriend. This male depends on the ministrations of his devoted, long-suffering girlfriend, who, as part of the plot, must be a student in one of my biology courses, which means that I too am part of the plot, serving as the dispassionate observer, and collateral victim, of a lopsided relationship.

This league of indigent boyfriends is remarkable because, at first blush, these males would seem to be capable of self-sufficiency: they are young, healthy, and brash. But, contrary to the laws of natural selection, these qualities do not appear to be enough to ensure survival. The truth is that they don't have cars, can't hold a job, and own cell phones that have been inactivated because they can't afford to pay for them. This means that their girlfriends own and maintain the cars, work overtime to support the relationship, and are constantly answering their cell phones in the middle of my class because their boyfriends are in need.

"I'm sorry," said one young lady as she gathered her things, still with the phone clamped between cheek and shoulder. "My boyfriend needs a ride to a job interview."

"I'm sorry I'm late," said another. "My boyfriend needed the car, so I had to walk."

"I have to leave early," apologized another in the middle of lab as she packed her cell phone into her bag. "My boyfriend hasn't eaten since breakfast and doesn't have any money to get food."

The only time I feel I might like to teach English is when I am listening to my students' stories. I imagine how I could help them harness their experiences to produce truly competent pieces of writing. Perhaps this is why I am impatient when I overhear them complaining about their creative writing classes and their difficulty getting started because of something they call "writer's block."

I don't believe in writer's block. I acknowledge that it is sometimes difficult to get started on a writing project (the late poet William Stafford compared sitting down to write to starting a car on wet ice). But I have absolutely no patience with writers like Henry Roth, who claimed to have been a victim of a sixty-year (!) bout of writer's block before producing his last novel, *A Diving Rock on the Hudson.*

And so I have sometimes been intrepid, perhaps rude, in inserting myself into my students' conversations when they protest that they don't know how to begin their writing assignments. "People!" I tell them. "Just think of your biology class and you'll be home free." In truth, if they could see it from my point of view, if they would just listen to what their peers tell me in the way of excuses for missed work, they would be privy to a bottomless pit of ideas, an encyclopedia of themes, a cornucopia of plot lines, a kaleidoscope of characters, motives, and denouements.

I once read somewhere that one's first thirteen years of life are a wellspring of inspiration: if ideas should ever escape you, look to your childhood. Yes, certainly, but it can't hold a candle to the experience of teaching college. The students roll in, wavelike, semester after semester, and their intentions and aspirations crash ceaselessly upon the shores of my expectations. The result is a stirring up of rationales to justify their inability to meet deadlines or to be even physically present. Because I cannot forestall these narratives, I listen, and note, and nod, saying, "It's okay." Then I leave it at that, and the students exit my office, still wondering where they stand.

I have sometimes toyed with the idea of writing fiction. I find that I can construct competent dialogue, create believable characters, and keep the action moving from A to B to C. But I can't seem to come up with a plot that is in any way singular. The reason: I think I have been poisoned, or trumped, by the narrative élan of my students. When I try to write fiction, I find myself thinking, "Well, a story about a priest who goes swimming at the Y to observe women's bodies is interesting, but how can it compare with Dan's story about his Saint Bernard falling through the river ice with his biology assignment in its jaws, or Lauren's about rushing home to retrieve her laboratory worksheet only to find her boyfriend in bed with another guy and having to drive three hundred miles to her mother's home in Madawaska for consolation?" All of this leads me to agree with those who have observed that there is no longer a need for fiction. Not in this world. Certainly not in the world of pedagogy.

All of the student anecdotes I have related swarm in my mind, like fireflies, blinking on and off. They have no fixity in time or place. I have forgotten exactly when they were given to me (and they are very real gifts to a writer) and, for the most part, who the givers were. But I am no less grateful for them, and I have offered them up here because I feel there is no risk of insult: I am pretty sure these erstwhile students have forgotten they ever said such things. In other words, these stories are in the public domain, part of the common wealth.

But there is one story that stands out above and beyond all the others, for its uniqueness, its power, and the dispassionate and unapologetic way it was delivered to me. It must be at least fifteen years ago by now. She was an older student. Perhaps thirty-eight. Poor. Drove a crummy car. Worked doggedly at biology, but it was clear that it didn't come easy to her. Up until the last quarter of the semester she had taken every quiz, every test, and handed in every assignment on time. Solid B work. Then she faltered. A missed test, a failed quiz, a string of absences. I called her in. "Is there something I need to know?" I asked.

She stood there, lank, with stringy, dirty blond hair, her expression worn. She gestured with her hand when she spoke, and I noted that it looked like a hand that was accustomed to holding a cigarette. "I need advice," she said, "because I know you have a boy. I have a son too. He's nine. The other night, while I was sleeping, he tried to set me on fire. Then he jumped out the second-floor window in his underwear into a snowdrift and ran off into the woods. What do you think I should do?"

I shook my head. Slowly. Then, conjuring the only words I thought appropriate, said, "I think you need to see a professional. Immediately."

She firmed her lip. "I did," she said, and I was struck by her lack of emotion throughout this telling, as if she were physically and mentally spent. "He told me to build a wooden box and put Adam in it for two hours a day."

I had no further advice for this unfortunate student. But I recall thinking, even if some psychologist did prescribe that unbelievable box therapy in earnest, how does one get a kid like that *into* the box?

That night I lay down beside my little boy as he made his transit through dreamland. The light of a full moon illuminated his room. My eyes wandered over to his bookshelves and I scanned the titles. The tales of Narnia, Oz, Musketeers, Tuck Everlasting . . . Who came up with such ideas? And why did they weave them into stories?

When I went to bed I had a dream about a single mother for whom life had gone hard, but she prevailed against the odds and got her associate's degree in five years. She couldn't have done it if her little boy had not been willing to take up the slack and become a little man at an early age. He helped around the house and comforted his mother when she was down. One evening, when she returned from a late class, the table was set with a simple meal — a pizza her son had made with a Boboli crust. When she went up on stage to take her diploma at the small December graduation ceremony, this nine-year-old cried, for he was sensitive beyond his years and perceived firsthand what his mother had been through, and that she had done it all for him as much as for herself. That evening they went home to their small, peel-paint house in the Maine woods and he lit a fire in the woodstove, before which they huddled as the drifts gathered in the dooryard and the wind howled about the eaves. And they lived happily ever after.

Any true story can be improved upon. I guess that's where fiction comes from. The fall semester begins in two weeks. ✤

our
common
tongue

whoa is the state of english

Perhaps it is the influence of e-mail, with its compression of language and penchant for abbreviation. Perhaps it is laziness. Perhaps it is the educational system itself, its ranks becoming increasingly filled with teachers who came of age in an era where appropriate English usage was deemphasized. Maybe it's a little bit of all of these, or maybe I'm making something out of nothing, like those UFO enthusiasts with their bumper stickers that read, THEY'RE HERE, AND THEY'RE AMONG US.

At this point, it has become almost hackneyed to decry the degradation of American English, especially as spoken by college students, who, we believe, should know better. As such, I run the risk of sounding like a fuddy-duddy when I resurrect this lament. The truth is, I don't talk about it very much at my college, where, as at all colleges and universities, the students' spoken English has been reduced to a collection of monosyllables punctuated by "like," "you know," and "whoa." As a college teacher, I am awash in a sea of such meaningless language, making any consideration of a counterattack an exercise in futility. Since there is little to no hope of making a dent among my own students, I have taken the last refuge of the frustrated: I have turned my attention to my own family, recognizing that charity—and torture—begin at home.

So far as I know, I am the only parent who still corrects his children's English. When my son Alyosha was ten and I did so, he would examine me with a questioning eye, as if he were viewing an oddity—a father who makes remarks about something that, in our culture, no longer seems to matter.

I think the breaking point that launched me upon my Molly Hatchet campaign came when I ran into one of my former students on campus, fresh from two months in Europe. This nineteen-year-old, who had never ventured farther than the borders of her home state, had had the opportunity of a lifetime. Being a traveler myself, and knowing how hard it was for me to shut up when I returned with my head brimming with impressions and experiences, I was full of anticipation when I asked her, "So, how was it?"

She nodded three or four times, searched the heavens for the right words, and then informed me, "It was, like, whoa."

And that was it. The glory of Greece and the grandeur of Rome summed up in a non-statement. My student's whoa was exceeded only by my head-shaking woe.

As a biology teacher perhaps I shouldn't be overly concerned with my students' English. After all, the traditional means of assessment in the sciences is the hated multiple choice exam, where students are asked to recognize, but not generate, language. My English-teaching colleagues are, however, duty-bound to extract essays and compositions and position papers from their charges. These products, I am told, are becoming increasingly awful.

Some of the problem sources (e-mail, TV, cell phones, etc.) are well known. But there is also something deeper. It is the way in which English, as opposed to other tongues, is viewed by Americans in general. In short, Americans consider French to be a language, as well as German, Italian, Chinese, and Swahili. But English is looked upon as the stuff that dribbles out when you open your mouth. As such, Americans are of two minds about English: on the one hand, they believe that it has a certain right of way, as evidenced by the uncomfortable sight of monoglot Americans traveling abroad, trying to communicate with foreigners. If they are not understood, they simply shout, the assumption being that anyone can understand English; it's only a question of volume.

On the other hand, Americans don't pay much attention to English because they just don't believe it matters so long as their meaning is grasped by the listener or reader.

The problems with these points of view are legion. I'd like to point out a few of the most egregious.

First, the habitual use of diseased English cuts one off from the conversation of many of the things that truly enrich life. These are: literature, music, science, even the daily newspaper. A student of mine once asked me if I had seen an article about a musical event being staged in a war-torn region of the world. "Isn't it nice," he commented, "that in the middle of all that mess someone is making music?" Then he showed me the headline: PANDEMONIUM IN MIDDLE EAST.

Second, lack of knowledge and appreciation of the structure of one's own language makes it all but impossible to learn a foreign one. If someone does not know what a noun is, or what is meant by "tense" or "case," how can one ever come to grips with the far more intricate grammars of other tongues? Once a student is confronted with parts of speech, let alone the subjunctive mood, the inclination is to give up, or, at best, learn a pidginized version of a foreign language: "*Yo* Tarzan, *tú* Jane." The result is inevitable frustration and a shoring up of one's belief that English is the "best" language and it is the duty of the rest of the world to learn it.

Third, without grammatical rules of the road to fall back on, students are dependent upon parroting what they see and hear around them. This makes formal transmission of the English language extremely difficult because teachers who speak poor English have no rules at their disposal when questions are posed by struggling students.

Fourth, the habituation of incorrect English takes a toll on teachers. I still recall a colleague who burst into my office one day in a sweat of panic. "Quick!" she commanded. "A dictionary!"

I watched as she tore through the book. "Just as I thought!" she exclaimed, pinning the entry with her finger. "It *is* spelled r-e-c-*e*-i-v-e."

Her point, whether she knew it or not, was that students make the same mistakes over and over, and their teachers read hundreds and eventually thousands of these repeat errors, which in time become more familiar than the accepted forms, so that the instructors themselves become tainted, uncertain whether it's rec*ie*ve or rec*ei*ve, prot*ie*n or prot*ei*n.

Fifth, a conscious investment in one's language is an investment in one's culture. I live in the poorest section of my Maine town. When important issues come before the town council, my neighbors are the ones conspicuous by their absence, even if an issue impacts them directly. Why? They feel outclassed because they fear they could never find the "right words" to express their feelings. (On occasion, though, one of my neighbors has shown up, and has found the right words, but I cannot print them here.) One cannot foster change, or defend one's interests, if one cannot articulate a point of view.

In light of these five points alone, the one thing that stories about the demise of English in America have in common is that they're all true. And students usually bear the brunt of the infamy, because there is a sense that they are somehow letting everybody down. The truth is that they are being misled everywhere they look and listen. Supermarket aisles point them to the "stationary," even though the pads and notebooks are not nailed down; people "could care less," even when they couldn't; and, more and more, friends and loved ones announce that they've just "ate" when, in fact, they've just eaten. Sloppy, sloppy, sloppy. Such carelessness promotes a culture of linguistic ignorance and laissez faire, creating a flume expediting the speaker all the way down to the swamp of language incompetence—the land of "like," "whoa," and "you know."

Blame must be laid somewhere, and I am happy to volunteer to place it squarely on the schools, which should be safe harbors and standard bearers for the sacred cause of correct English usage. Instead, they don't teach grammar at all (however, I have of late seen a pilot light of effort in the lower grades). Or syntax. In fact, the younger teachers themselves seem to have little knowledge of these underpinnings of the language, because they also went without exposure to it.

The thing is, it takes so little to get language back on track. One does not have to return to the days of diagramming sentences (although, what was wrong with that?); but rather than assign eight papers in a class, why not only three, each of which is slowly but surely mentored to perfection through repeated revisions? In academia, there are few things as satisfying as being able to place successive drafts of one's work side-by-side and note the visible progress, like those charts of the stages of human evolution, where the hairy quadruped gradually gets on its feet and becomes proud, fire-making *Homo erectus* and finally the handsome *Homo sapiens*. It's a long haul, but in the end it's worth it. (At least you get your nose off the ground.)

I realize that many teachers, especially college teachers, will protest that this is exactly what they are doing. If so, then the trick is to make the jump to warp speed by translating writing competence to speaking competence. This is something I know the schools aren't doing. And so, their having affirmed poor or sloppy speech habits through their lack of attention to them, I am obligated to do the dirty work of gently ushering my kids onto the path of competent communication. But, as the Wicked Witch of the West said in one of her rhetorical musings, "These things must be handled delicately" (my sons' patience is limited when Dad behaves like a teacher).

I recall one day when Alyosha was little and we were driving to a nearby town. As we set out on our five-mile trip, he noticed a crow in eccentric flight and said, "It's flying so raggedly." Impressed with his description, I remarked, "Good adverb!"

Alyosha asked me what an adverb was. I explained that it's a word that tells you something about a verb. Which led to his asking me what a verb is. I explained that it's an action word, giving him the example, *Dad drives the truck.* "*Drives* is the verb," I told him, "because it's the thing Dad is doing."

Alyosha became intrigued with the idea of action words. So we listed a few more. "Fly," "swim," "dive," "run." And then, having fallen prey to his own curiosity, he asked me if other words had names. This led to a discussion about nouns, adjectives, and articles. The upshot of all this is that within the span of a ten-minute drive, Alyosha had learned — from scratch — to recognize the major parts of speech in a sentence.

It was painless and fun, but it's not being effectively taught in the elementary and high schools, which means that the colleges are the recipients of students who not only cannot communicate, but cannot comprehend the communications of others, especially when it comes to literature and textbooks. Again, students project the sense that as long as they are making themselves understood, all is well. Sort of like driving a junker that blows smoke and has a flat tire: if it gets you there, what's the problem?

Perhaps, then, language should be looked upon as a possession: keeping it clean and in repair shows concern and effort. It demonstrates attentiveness to detail and the always satisfying accomplishment of a goal—clear, accurate, descriptive speech.

Not long after spotting that crow, Alyosha and I were eating breakfast together when I attempted to add milk to my tea. "Dad," he cautioned, "if I were you I wouldn't do that. It's sour."

"Alyosha," I said, swelling with pride, "that's a grammatically perfect sentence. You used 'were' instead of 'was.'"

"I know, I know," he said with a degree of weary irritation. "It's the subjunctive mood."

I was, like, whoa. ⚘

the illiterati

It's hard to imagine a time when information was not transmitted electronically. Charles Dickens, for example, serialized his novels in British magazines, which were then shipped by freighter to America. That part of the process alone took several weeks. A story is told of the final installment of his novel *The Old Curiosity Shop*, which is about the travails of a girl child (Little Nell) and the grandfather who loves and cares for her. As the climax of the story approaches, the girl becomes gravely ill. Americans, having read the penultimate installment, had to endure the agony of waiting for a ship to bring news of Little Nell's fate to our shores. As the freighter approached the port of New York, desperate mobs—frantic with concern—crowded the pier, screaming out to the ship, "Did Little Nell live? Did she *live*?"

(She did not.)

Whether this anecdote is apocryphal is beside the point. It is a good story with a valuable lesson about a time when the only means of conveying information over distance was to write it down and send it—by foot courier, horseman, ship, or carrier pigeon.

The Bible says, "In the beginning was the Word." How true. I am mindful of a story related by Sven Birkerts in his book *The Gutenberg Elegies* (subtitled "The Fate of Reading in an Electronic Age"). He describes daily life in sixteenth-century Europe, a time when few people could read and as a result there were few books. Those who were literate might own only three volumes: an almanac (so that they would know when to plant), a devotional of some sort (so that they would know how to pray), and a Bible. Only the very literate—mostly churchmen—ventured beyond these few works.

Birkerts goes on to describe how the Renaissance humanist Erasmus of Rotterdam was out walking one day when he suddenly froze in his tracks. He had spotted a scrap of paper on the ground with printing on it (this was a time when there were no newspapers and street and shop signs were all but non-existent, because almost nobody could read them). Imagine that. A few printed words were enough to elicit a sense of wonder in an educated man. (Birkerts gives no indication of what that piece of paper actually said.)

I refer to these stories about Dickens and Erasmus because they highlight, for me, an obvious truth and a towering irony: we live in an illiterate age.

How can this be? There are more books in and out of print than at any time in history. Newspapers and magazines abound. E-mail has become ubiquitous. But confluent with these print media are strictly image-laden and auditory sources of information: videos, movies, cell phones, computer graphics, iPods, and, of course, television the damned. The problem I am grappling with is the supplantation of the printed word by the visual image and the spoken word, and the devastating effect this has had upon my students' ability to comprehend and interpret written information in a literate way.

In 2004, the National Endowment for the Arts released a study of Americans' reading habits. A survey of 17,135 people showed a steep — and accelerating — decline in the number of readers, especially young readers, since 1992. In addition, only 57 percent of Americans admitted to having read a book *of any kind* in the previous year. I note with curiosity and wonder that 1992 was the year the World Wide Web was getting its flight wings.

I run the risk here of sounding shocked. I'm not. As a teacher, I know that the lack of my students' book knowledge is exceeded only by their lack of any *desire* to read. Once again, the principal culprit is the almost total replacement of the written word by the predigested, simplified, pasteurized, and transmogrified (did I miss an adjective?) pap of visual media. (How many times have I asked a student if he or she had read a particular book, only to be told, with confidence, "No, but I saw the movie"?) Is it any wonder that Americans have gone from historically treating their politicians with skepticism if not ire to venerating them as prophets, thanks to the non-stop "enlightenment" offered by the boob tube? (In a recent survey of the citizenry, Ronald Reagan was voted "the greatest American.")

When the mass production of books finally got underway in the seventeenth century, it not only sated a thirst for printed matter, but stimulated it as well. By the time Thomas Paine wrote his incendiary pamphlet, "Common Sense," at the outset of the American Revolution, the power of the written word to stir passions *en masse* was well established. It is difficult to imagine anyone getting worked up over a book today. Any book. (Let's leave the Bible, the Koran and Harry Potter out of this for now). Especially fiction, which has nothing on the realities of the American social and political scenes. But is this why Americans are steadily giving up on reading? Is American life itself simply far more interesting than any creation of an author's pen?

Possibly. But mostly it is the seduction of visual imagery and the quintessentially American taste for the quick fix (auto tune-ups in a can; diet pills; internet Ph.D.s; exercises that can be done in one's sleep, etc.). Why read a newspaper when Dan Rather can summarize a war in thirty seconds, complete with instructions on how we should feel about it? Why read a book detailing life in a past century when our leaders tell us that history is irrelevant because we are living in "special" times that cannot benefit from the experiences and wisdom of those who went before us? The "need to know" is satisfied by the sound bite, the video clip, the talking head.

However, when we substitute a movie for a book, what we lose, of course, is nuance and subtext. In reading, we grapple not only with raw information, but with the writer's style and intent. Reading is a joining of minds, often an intellectual battle between reader and writer. Engaging a challenging book is nothing less than working up a good sweat at the mental gym.

Oof, I'm already working up that sweat. But I'm far from finished. Remember: I'm a teacher, and as such I bear much of the brunt of my students' illiteracy. In the interest of showing some mercy, I'll admit that some students are "simply" functionally illiterate—they can read, but not interpret, information in a textbook. But there are others in the ranks for whom words are opaque symbols, like the curlicues of alien language purportedly found on the wreckage of that UFO at Roswell.

Some examples. I was once teaching a section on genetics in my general biology course. At one point, I uttered the following: "Gregor Mendel's early work on the nuts and bolts of heredity was superlative." After class a young woman approached me. She told me she was really struggling to take notes. I asked her if I was speaking too fast. She shook her head. "No," she said. "It's all those big words you use. Like 'supertive.'" [sic]

This is important. You see, students struggle with understanding scientific ideas not so much because they are complicated, but rather because they don't understand the everyday English used to convey them, which is a far more serious problem. I can accept that students may be confounded by the statement, "Polychaetes have lateral parapodia," because they don't yet know what polychaetes are (they're worms). But their deficiency is far more rudimentary—they don't know what "lateral" means, and so the entire language is the enemy, erecting an enormous rampart against learning.

Reading, of course, is the best way to increase one's vocabulary, because a reading vocabulary is larger than a speaking one. (The German word for vocabulary is *Wortschatz*—word treasure.) If one is a conscientious and observant reader, one learns how to judiciously incorporate new words and expressions into one's speech. Thus, when Thoreau writes, "We are double-edged blades, and every time we whet our virtue the return stroke strops our vice," the student may get snagged on the word "strops," but only for a moment. With dictionary at hand, the mystery can be immediately resolved. But even without a dictionary, one can often gain an understanding of a previously unknown word from its context. Here, in Thoreau's quote, if the student can imagine the back and forth sharpening of a blade on a flap of leather (a strop), the meaning has a good chance of making itself known at first blush. Strop. What a wonderful coin to add to one's *Wortschatz*.

Reading, therefore, is a game. And like any game, one gets better at it until the process becomes automatic, and, one hopes, addictive. But without reading, one becomes divorced from the conversation of educated humankind. In concrete terms, if one does not read, one acquires little facility with English idiomatic expression and one's speech becomes flat, repetitive, and one-dimensional.

By way of illustration, I'd like to recall the case of a student I had many years ago. Her name was Melissa. She sat in the far left-hand corner of the room and was not doing well. I finally took her aside. She told me she didn't understand most of what I was saying, so she didn't take notes. "Do you read the text?" I asked. She shook her head. "I don't like to read."

Hmm. I asked her if she was frustrated. She said yes, she was, but not for the reason she had cited. Instead, she named another student in the class, one who was doing superlative (!) work. "I don't see how she gets A's all the time. She never says anything."

"Well," I said, "still waters run deep."

Melissa made eyes at me. "What do you mean?" she asked.

"Well, you know, sometimes quiet people have very active minds."

Melissa slowly nodded, then said, "Yeah, but what does that have to do with water?"

The moral here is that reading is a means of preserving and transmitting English idiom—the stylistic way that language is used. Idioms and expressions and metaphors and similes and symbols are expressive tools, and reading is a way of learning not only to recognize them, but also to use them. If my students lack any recognition of these things, then I, as a teacher, am reduced to pidginizing my speech. I would like to be able to say, in response to a middling quiz grade, "There's no use crying over spilled milk," but, believe it or not, there are those who would be thrown by this expression. And so I must rephrase: "What's done is done. Let's move on." The same meaning, but it's the idea that I *must* be so literal that stirs in me a sense of loss.

Reflective of this, I once assigned a reading to my students by the late evolutionary biologist Stephen Jay Gould, called "The Lesson of the Dinosaurs: Evolution Didn't Inevitably Lead to Us." Gould points out that the most reasonable explanation for the extinction of the dinosaurs was a meteoric impact; in his words, "the ultimate bolt from the blue." In an accompanying question sheet, I asked, "To what does Gould attribute the extinction of the dinosaurs?" A few days later, when the papers came back, here were some of the responses:

- "a blue lightning bolt"
- "something blue"
- "something blew them away"

Few of the students had ever heard the expression, "like a bolt from the blue." I therefore had to reduce Gould's elegant use of idiom to: "a meteor hit the planet," so everyone would be on the same page.

Sad.

An interesting sidelight of all this is that many, many students who do not read, write. And what they write is poetry, of all things. But they don't read any poetry, and as a result, what they write is abysmal because they don't really know what poetry is.

Once, while walking through the hallway of my building, I found a student, a young woman, sitting against the wall with her legs crossed, writing languidly in a notebook. Like Erasmus and his scrap of paper, I stopped and stared. "What are you writing?" I asked.

She looked up at me, dreamy-eyed, and whispered, "Poetry."

"Oh," I said. "I love poetry." And, in a bid to kindle a conversation, I asked, "Have you ever read Robert Frost?"

The young poet firmed her lip, thought for a moment, and said, "No. Who is he?"

I smiled and readjusted the books under my arm. "A forgotten poet," I said, and moved on.

Ach, I am not only a nostalgic. I am a romantic. Worse, according to the National Endowment for the Arts, I am becoming a dinosaur. Who today would agree with Erasmus, who said, "Whenever I have a little money I buy books; if any is left, I buy food and clothing"?

I now understand why McDonald's continues its imperial expansion throughout the world, while public libraries are being closed for lack of funds. ♠

the written word

I once heard a story about the time, during the Civil War, that a distraught mother went to the White House to beseech Abraham Lincoln to help her discern the fate of her son, a teenage foot soldier, from whom she hadn't heard in months. Lincoln immediately dispatched an officer, who located the boy on one of the fronts and escorted him back to Washington. Standing before the president (and quivering with fear, one may assume), the boy waited for the commander-in-chief to speak. Lincoln finally looked up from his desk and uttered three words: "Write your mother."

Current information technology renders such anecdotes quaint. We live in an age when the written letter is no longer our solitary, desperate link to home and hearth. Soldiers in active combat in far-flung corners of the world have access to telephones and the Internet ("Came under mortar attack today, but otherwise fine. Tell Caleb not to forget to feed Trixie"). From the standpoint of the well-being of the English language, this is exactly the problem. In contrast to ages past, when the only way to communicate information over distance was to write it down and send it by physical means, most information today is communicated orally and aurally. The phone call has replaced the written letter. Television continues to make inroads against newspapers. Even a cell phone can transmit an image — worth a thousand words of pecked-out text.

There really is, in practical terms, no longer much of a need to write. My students know this, and therefore balk at my giving writing assignments (and demanding quality to boot). Am I a relic of an antique age? Well, yes, I am, but I persist for a good reason: I believe that written language matters; which begs the question, why don't my students?

The most salient reason is that students believe they can function just fine without writing, thereby erecting a barrier of apathy that, for the instructor, makes teaching writing as thankless a task as collecting tolls on the New Jersey Turnpike.

Second, many courses do not require that students write. Math, for one. And most science classes. I have even seen history and—gulp—literature courses where assessments were done with multiple choice tests, in which students must learn simply to recognize correct answers, but do not have to generate written information of their own. This conveys the message that, if most courses place no emphasis on student writing, those that do are being, somehow, punitive.

Third, in the last thirty years or so, writing has been de-emphasized in the elementary and high schools (although it may be making a comeback, as evidenced by the new essay portion of the SAT), in favor of better-funded technology education, and the abomination of "creative spelling" and "creative language," in which students are allowed—even encouraged—to proceed down labyrinths of error-ridden language in the belief that they will learn to extricate themselves "later on" (after their mangled grammars, spellings, and syntaxes have become habituated).

Last, students, by and large, do not read. They therefore have little familiarity with good writing. The result is that, when they do write something, they become indignant (if they care at all) when it comes back to them with copious corrections and/or a poor grade, since they believe that anything they have troubled themselves to write must, by virtue of their efforts, be good, or at least acceptable. (Moral: in order to write well you must read well.)

The task, then, is to give students reasons to want to write, and to write clearly, concisely, and purposefully. Let me begin by quoting some famous authors on the reasons they write.

John Ashbery, American poet: "I write to find out what I'm thinking." This is an immensely important and insightful comment. How many times have you sat down to write a letter, or even an e-mail, and discovered how one thought prompts another, like a fall of dominoes? No one ever has the full text of a story, essay, or even a letter in his head before he begins to create it. Writing is something that happens on paper (or the computer screen).

Isaac Bashevis Singer, Nobel laureate: "Literature is the memory of humanity." When we write, we make a contribution to a larger narrative, humbly offering up a view from our tiny, troglodytic corner of the human experience. I'll never forget the solitary line of a schoolboy's poem, cited by E. B. White in his essay "Homecoming," which has special meaning for me as a resident of Maine. It has to do with a small, gently flowing river, the Narramissic (what a beautiful word), not far from my home. The boy wrote, "It flows through Orland every day." Every time I cross the small Narramissic River bridge, I slow the car and recite this line aloud, whether I am alone or not. The pleasing wavelets of its cadence never fail to stir me (as they did E. B. White, who commented, "I never cross that mild stream without thinking of [that schoolboy's] testimonial to the constancy, the dependability, of small, familiar rivers"). If not for this kid's modest statement, humanity would have been deprived of a record of a child's view of the Narramissic.

Jay McInerney, novelist (best work, *Bright Lights, Big City*): "Writers write because they don't move easily in the world as it is." Wow. That's exactly it. Everyone wishes that the world would operate exactly the way he wants it to. But it can't. Except when you write. That's where you lay down the ground rules, make characters behave the way you want them to, and exact the justice you're convinced you've been denied all your life. When you write, you create a world of your own, and you are its absolute master. What a privilege. What power.

If, through the use of such quotes, and other legerdemain, I can bring my students to the threshold of the *desire* to write, the question they often raise is, "What do I write about?" The answer is obvious, and it has been repeated so often and by so many writers that I am ashamed to regurgitate it here; but I must: write about what you know.

I suppose it is possible for a twenty-year-old who never left Wytopitlock, Maine, to write a novel about the adventures of a warrior maiden in medieval Albania, but it probably wouldn't ring true. (There are exceptions! Karl May, for example, was a German who never visited the American West, but became wildly famous for his stories about cowboys and Indians.) Writing is a sensual act. How would our imaginary author describe the smells of the Albanian forest primeval? The colors of the North Albanian Alps at sunset as the heroine gazes out over the Shkumbin River from Elbasan? The caress of a sex-crazed monk from Rrogozhinë, said to drive women to the farthest reaches of ecstasy?

When one writes about one's own experiences, one's language is more charged. Our finest writers bear this out. Think of Mark Twain's tales of boyhood, his descriptions of the mercantile culture of the Mississippi. Or Joseph Conrad's penetrating melodramas of human desperation on the high seas. Flannery O'Connor's character portraits. But there's also the mundane. I never fail to smile when I read, and re-read, Robert Frost's poems, which have become, over the years, old friends. His topics? A balled-up newspaper in a snowdrift. A road covered with leaves. Rose pogonias. A birch tree. A mouse. And every one of these pieces, because of its deft use of language drawn from the author's own experiences, is, to me, as powerful as the *Sturm und Drang* of Conrad's *Typhoon*, with its howling winds and frantic mariners.

Several years ago I was invited to do a week-long stint as a writer-in-residence at a high school in southern Maine. I leapt at the opportunity. After several days of presentations on such stock topics as editing and character development, I invited the students to meet with me one-on-one if they had something they wanted me to read. As with any large group, most of the work was average; but there were also shimmers of real talent.

One senior girl, Rebecca, brought a short story. Quietly and without preamble, she handed it to me and then took a desk seat. As I read it, the hair stood up on the back of my neck. The piece was not only technically well done (proper spelling, well-constructed paragraphs, consistent tone, etc.), but electrifying. It was about a young woman who lives with an older sister who is insane. But this is not clear from the outset. The revelation of the sister's imbalance progresses like the falling dark, until the reader wants to jump to his feet and scream to the younger sibling to get the hell out of the house before it's too late.

After reading the story I looked up at Rebecca and asked, "Is this in any way autobiographical?" She nodded. So I went on to give her some unsolicited professional direction: "If writing is something you think you'd like to do as a career, I believe you'll be successful."

By contrast, another student, a young man, brought me a story about a town that is terrorized by flocks of birds that break through windows, bite people, and give them rabies. After reading the piece, I looked at the boy, his eyes filled with hope, and, ever so gently, told him that birds don't carry rabies. He became resentful, and I allowed him this. But the point here is that this type of work is what can usually be expected when one attempts to describe terra incognita.

Science writing is different, in that there is far less room for creativity; that is, one is restricted to an elucidation of the facts. But once again, the experiments my students carry out represent knowledge gained and become part of their personal experience. Having gotten a whiff of sulfur, having used a Bunsen burner, having manipulated the controls of a microscope, they become experts on these things. In short, I have relieved my students of the burden of having to figure out what to write about.

Which leads me to a second major problem that students have with writing of any sort: their lack of willingness to edit. Getting students to want to write can pale in comparison to motivating them to revise their work. Once again, this reflects their belief that anything they have taken pains to write must be acceptable, if not good, simply because they have troubled themselves to put it on paper.

The business of writing is rewriting. There is no successful writer who does not edit his work. The sainted E. B. White was famous for his disdain of the unnecessary word, pruning an essay until he had produced a triple-distilled ambrosia of seamless, and memorable, prose. The novelist John Irving (*The World According to Garp*) is said to be so obsessive about his writing that he hand-edits even his already-published books.

Revising is a lot like waxing a car. You apply a dollop of wax, and then, with a clean rag, slowly and deliberately, 'round and 'round you go, over and over again. With every pass a little more of the filmy wax disappears, until the car's finish shines through. Eventually, at a point that you alone can determine, you stand back, take a look at your work, and say, "There." (Even then, another observer might pass by and say, "You missed a spot." Don't be indignant. This is an unsolicited gift. Pick up your cloth and get back to work.)

In the laboratory section of my biology course, I require that my students write essays summarizing what they've learned. Science being science, the format is very strict, designed to help my students "stay within the lines," so to speak. There are always a few students in the class for whom the work is self-evident: they have a ready command of how language is structured, and they are aware enough of the reader to fill in all the blanks. Others, though, react as if I have asked them to excise their livers without benefit of anesthesia. It is as if they have never, in their lives, written anything more demanding than a shopping list.

Such was the case with a young man—dear and big-hearted, which makes this all the more painful to report—who had just completed a laboratory assignment on enzymes. In this experiment I had the students fill test tubes with spit (excuse me, saliva), add starch, and then, with benefit of a color-changing chemical indicator, observe how long it took for the enzyme (amylase) in the saliva to break the starch down to sugar. The first section of the assignment required that the students write down the purpose of the experiment. Here's what this student wrote: "My purpose, was to spitted, so that blue became orange."

I kid you not. The rest of the lab essay was equally appalling.

Although this student did not know it, he was at war with the English language. Wars are notoriously difficult to win in one fell swoop. Victory must be achieved battle-by-battle. Rather than risk alienating the student by telling him everything that was wrong with his writing, I decided to broach the problems one at a time, in rough order of ease of redress: spelling, grammar, completeness, accuracy, context, style. He stuck with me, listening intently as if I were divulging the secrets of the cabala. And slowly, but surely, his modest paragraph took form, until it became this: "My purpose was to see how Benedict's solution can demonstrate the ability of amylase to catalyze the breakdown of starch to sugar."

I didn't write this for him; he did it himself, with my hand on his shoulder. It took us an hour — working like Marie and Pierre Curie, who processed tons of pitchblende to come up with a speck of radium — to produce this pearl. But when we were done the student had acquired something even more lasting — a *sense* of language. His subsequent writing, which he did entirely on his own, wasn't perfect, but it was better. Because he now had a willingness to edit and revise, going 'round and 'round, until the wax, or most of it at least, had disappeared.

Once we have discovered what we want to write about, writing — and editing — are precious opportunities to think slowly about things. Writing is central to all disciplines, from English to math to biology to computer science. It is the glue. ♣

why e-mail is not writing

I remember once reading an article in a newspaper or magazine in which the writer rejoiced that American students, long lamented for their deteriorating writing skills, were now welling with promise because of e-mail. "It's a new literary renaissance," the writer gushed.

My response: Baloney.

When Jack Kerouac published *On the Road*, which he had written on a roll of toilet paper, Truman Capote famously sniffed, "That's not writing, it's typing."

With respect to e-mail, those are my sentiments exactly.

In the strict mechanical sense, of course e-mail is writing, if one defines writing merely as lining up symbols to convey a message. But if writing is defined as an art form or a skill that must be developed and honed, then e-mail is anything but. If e-mail were truly writing in this sense, then the professorial directive, "Write a story about such and such" could easily be replaced by, "Send me an e-mail about such and such."

I don't think I would bristle so if the evidence against e-mail as literature weren't staring me in the face. I'd like to put the ducks of my argument in a straight line. As preamble, one must agree to define writing as a skill or art rather than a simple mechanical act, in the same way that baseball is much more than just swinging a bat. Okay? Let's go.

Point number one. Writing is about structure.

Essays have their themes or premises; short stories and novels have their plots; poetry has its music and cadence; and non-fiction marches forward in some logical narrative fashion, sometimes with a counterpoint of argument and evidence. The question being begged then, is, where is e-mail's structure? The answer is that there is no one form that one must bear in mind while writing an e-mail and which defines it as a genre. E-mail is more like a garage sale. See for yourself:

EXAMPLE #1:
> Hey Dude:
> C-U @ 4. U gt the note? (LOL) :) — Butch

EXAMPLE #2:
> Dear Adam:
> Where shall I begin? I don't like writing e-mails, but you leave me little choice, since you won't anser [*sic*] the phone. I thought I knew you, but when I saw you with Crystal Jakobowski down in the gravel pit I realized that I didn't really know you at all. WHY DON"T YOU PICK UP THE PHONE WHEN I CALL??!! — Debbie

EXAMPLE #3:
> To All Colleagues in the College of Arts & Sciences:
> The meeting to discuss the budget for the new fiscal year will include a new agenda item: whether to put the new sidewalk on the Goins Hall side of campus or on the side where the salt shed is located. This promises to be a very exciting meeting, so please plan to attend. Refreshments will be served.

E-mail clearly has no defining form; therefore it is not writing.

Point number two. E-mail, being electronic,
is not perceived as real. The result: sloppiness.

When the Sumerians used a stylus to press cuneiform into clay tablets, that was real. When someone uses a pen to put wet ink on paper, that is real. Braille is real. But what exactly are those illuminated letters on a computer monitor? Not only can we not feel them, not only do they not smear or stain our fingers, but with the touch of the "delete" key we can make them disappear. E-mail is cheap to produce, requires little effort (no paper to fold, no stamps to lick, etc.), and conveys the sense that once the "send" key is pushed the "message" somehow evaporates into that ether occupied by the universal dust and unmatched socks. Because of this ethereal quality, we tend to be sloppy with e-mail. In fact, I would go so far as to suggest that sloppiness is the defining quality of e-mail. But sloppiness is *precisely* what one seeks to avoid in real writing. Therefore, e-mail is not writing.

Point number three. Who edits e-mail?

The business of writing is rewriting. There is no successful writer who does not go at his work with pickaxe and shovel until he has worked it into acceptable shape. A very common approach among writers is to get a draft down on paper (or the computer screen), put it away for a day or days, then take it out again and look at it with new eyes, then edit. Sometimes a writer will repeat this several times before sending his work out. And then some editor will almost always comb through the work again. The object is to produce something that, at the very least, is free of typographical and structural errors; at best, something both writer and publisher can be proud of.

But who edits e-mail? The whole point of e-mail is speed. The very idea of being able to transmit a message at near-light velocity fosters a simple two-step of typing and sending, typing and sending. This is why e-mail is so poorly written: it's more of a memo system than a means of producing finished work. Who labors for days over an e-mail message, working on such things as subtext, character development, and plot? I have never received one that was anything other than a barebones way to tell me something. E-mail is not a form that emphasizes quality; therefore it is not writing.

Point number four. Where are the anthologies of collected e-mails?

Literary history is rife with authors' (and common folks') collected letters. Think of John Adams, C. S. Lewis, George Bernard

Shaw (who, in 1891, wrote in his diary, "This correspondence is getting intolerable"). What defines these missives is the care with which they were written, the sentiments they contain, and how they reflect the times in which they were penned. In other words, in contrast to e-mail, which, as I previously stated, is perceived as unreal, letters have tangible permanence. One tends to be more careful about what one writes in a letter, for two reasons: one, writing on paper is a fairly slow process, affording one a better chance of arriving at the right words. Two, every letter has a distinct character — the paper, the envelope, the stamp, the saliva, not to mention the contents. For anyone who has ever written a letter, especially with a pen, just as he or she hovers with it over the slot of the mailbox, there is the conscious or subconscious sense of the possibility that it will be saved by its recipient.

E-mails, by contrast, are assumed to be destined for the delete key after being read. No permanence is involved, therefore little care is taken to make them anything special. There are no anthologies titled "The Collected E-mails of So-and-So" because no one seems to be writing e-mails worth saving. Since e-mail is not considered a written form worth preserving, it is not writing.

Last point. E-mail lends itself to speed,
which is fatal to the writer's critical eye.

I once read something — I think it came to me in an e-mail — about the process of writing, to wit: if you compose on a computer, revise in pencil (somewhere in the process, make it slow). But who would even think of doing such a thing with e-mail? E-mail's entire convenience lies in its speed, and few things done in haste (think of fast food) are prized for their quality. Writing is certainly no exception.

In the biology courses I teach at my small, impoverished, careworn college in central Maine, I demand a lot of writing from my students. Hard copy. On paper. But because e-mail is now used by everyone, it has promoted a culture of procrastination because work can be drafted and sent out in a twinkling, even as deadlines loom like thunderheads. One result is that I am seeing more and more students who wait until the last moment before sitting down to write their assignments. (Yes, yes, I know that students have always crammed, even before the advent of computers. But the result was something that had to be handed to the instructor in a prescribed format and was therefore usually presentable.) To buy as much time as possible, students ask if they can e-mail their assignments to me. If I say yes, they sigh with relief. And then, on the day the assignment is due, they run to a computer, peck out their work in e-mail form, close their eyes and hit "send." It's up to me to access the e-mail and, if I want a hard copy, print it out in my office. I have never received an e-mail assignment that was exemplary. Moral: E-mail is a means of quickly drafting and sending information. This is messaging, which is not writing.

I once presented my criticism of e-mail-as-writing when I was the keynote speaker at an educational conference aimed at teachers interested in getting their students to improve their writing. I wouldn't have said a thing about e-mail if I hadn't been asked, because it just didn't seem valuable in my mind. The questioner was one of the organizers. He was also an adherent of the view that e-mail is a wonderful way for students to get involved with writing.

After lowering the boom of my response on this man, point upon point, I felt that I had wounded him in some way, because he sat there staring at me with an open mouth. I tried to patch things up a bit by adding, in afterthought, "This is only my personal view. I might be wrong, and I'm certainly willing to think about it." (To no avail. I was never invited back.)

In the interim, I have thought about it. But I find that I cannot give any ground in my belief that e-mail has done nothing to improve the overall quality of student writing in either our high schools or colleges. E-mail is a great tool, and it's fun and fast, but if it were somehow an innovative way for students to improve their written work, then the question being begged is this: are teachers using e-mail *in a deliberate way* to develop their students' writing?

So far as I know, they are not. Whatever advantage or benefit they see in their students' use of e-mail is more of a passive or anecdotal observation that anyone who relentlessly pecks out information on a keyboard *must* be getting better at writing. But without the instructor's oversight and direction, and without a willingness to edit one's "work," e-mail, in this regard, is about as helpful in developing written language skills as is eating bowl after bowl of alphabet soup. ♣

i write, therefore i'm right

Nothing grants insight into a student's understanding of a concept like asking him or her to write about it. During class, when I pause to ask, "Do you understand this?" the response is either a blank stare or a nod, both to me and the painfully slow-ticking clock on the wall. This ambiguous response tells me nothing except that the student wants me to go on with the lecture, as if my pausing to elucidate a concept will suspend time and delay the much-anticipated end of the class period.

Students do not generally come into a science course expecting to write much of anything, save for the occasional essay question on a test. In fact, science is so terminology-heavy that it lends itself to multiple choice tests and short answers as a way of covering as much ground as possible. And yet, students will normally do what is asked of them, even if grudgingly.

In this light, I ask them to write, at length, their observations and interpretations of their laboratory experiments. I prescribe the format, akin to a step-by-step recipe, but still it is a long, difficult slog for many. There are two reasons for this: students don't like to write; and, more toxically, they tend to believe that anything that does manage to flow from their pens — or keyboards — is valid.

Here's how it works. After each lab session I hand out a sheet outlining what I want to see in their write-ups. The format is as follows: Title. Purpose. Materials. Procedure. Results. Discussion. Conclusion. Everything — *everything* — except for the discussion is matter-of-fact and does not require them to think. The *Purpose* is a simple statement of what they intended to find out ("I wanted to see how the sow bug responded to light"). The *Materials* section is simply a list of what they used (glassware, light source, sow bugs, etc.). The *Results* are just the facts: what they found out ("The sow bug always moves away from the light"). But the *Discussion* is where the students get to shine. This is the heart and soul of the laboratory write-up, because it is, in itself, an essay that explains their understanding of their results. And it is precisely here, in the discussion, that the students run their ships onto the rocks. But their Results section also provides its share of drama, because, once they get rolling, the students cannot resist the temptation to move beyond the facts and into the realm of speculation, or worse, how they "feel" about the sow bug's experience, or worst of all, how the sow bug might feel.

Let me put all of this in context with a concrete example. Take the topic of photosynthesis (the means by which plants convert sun energy to food energy, releasing oxygen along the way). As part of the laboratory exercise on this topic, the students place a sprig of an aquatic plant in a test tube filled with sodium bicarbonate solution, shine a light on it, and measure the amount of oxygen given off. Simple enough. The Results section should simply include numbers (the amount of oxygen produced), and students do okay here if they remember to stay on the straight and narrow and not stray beyond the facts. But, alas, stray they do. It's as if the facts (my plant produced X amount of oxygen) are not good enough, or don't seem to say enough. And so they give in to temptation and add heaps of qualifiers to their data ("This was amazing! Who thought that a plant could produce oxygen? I was blown away by the results!"). Of course, I edit all of this fluff out with admonishments such as, "Stick to the facts," and "Describe only what you saw, not how you feel about it."

This is a problem. For college students, especially the younger ones fresh out of high school, it's all about feelings. If you doubt this, ask an English professor who directs his or her students to keep journals. Even when the students are asked to, say, identify an aspect of a piece of literature and then comment on it, their commentaries are far and away longer and grander than anything that might be termed objective. And it's more often than not deeply personal. It's as if they have channeled Emerson, who wrote, "to believe that what is true for you in your private heart is true for all men — that is genius." And who am I, or any teacher, to correct the work of a genius?

Be that as it may, it is a semester-long battle to get my students to write down their results without all the trimmings. I often get a sense that, in correcting their work, they feel that I am being unfair, unkind, or even cruel.

A recurring feature of their Results section is the use of the word "interesting" as a proxy for data. Instead of writing, for example, "When I placed the plant in the dark, it ceased photosynthesis but continued to undergo cell respiration," I see, "This experiment was very interesting." The problem is that the word "interesting" does not convey any information. It is the ultimate useless word because it can mean anything and therefore means nothing. I tell this to my students firmly and clearly, but despite my admonition, they hang onto this word with grim determination. One student used it repeatedly, like the "stop" fragment in a telegram. When I crossed out all her "interesting"s, she drove to my house in a howling rainstorm and angrily shook the rolled-up paper at me. "You're trying to cut me down!" she shouted. "No,"

I countered, "I'm trying to help you improve your writing" (all the while asking myself why I was standing in the rain having a debate about a word I considered useless).

If the Results sections of my students' write-ups are problematic, that's child's play when compared with the lengthier and more demanding Discussion, where they are supposed to detail their understanding of the topic by interpreting their data. The first few times they are confronted with a discussion, the students' minds go, to quote a Robert Frost poem, "every which way in the joints." For them, embarking upon a discussion is akin to taking the training wheels off one's bike: it's wobbly. Very wobbly.

The main problem, again, is emotionalism (actually, I like former Federal Reserve chairman Alan Greenspan's language better, when he described the run-up in the prices of tech stocks back in the 1990s, calling it "irrational exuberance"). Students, perhaps because they don't trust their understanding of the facts of their experiments, substitute unchained language for data. For example, in the discussion of photosynthesis, it would be valid to write, "oxygen was produced at a rate of 0.2 cc per minute," and then go on to explain the significance of this. But what I often see is, "It was amazing that gas actually came out of the plant. It was like it was breathing!" Or, as a budding English major wrote, "This lab had a grim, stultifying aspect to it, inhibiting my desire to see it through. However, persist I did." Other words that serve as useless ballast and substitutions for real information are "awesome," "incredible," "great," "fascinating" and, in one instance, "scintillating" (the student was referring to the electrolytic separation of water into hydrogen and oxygen).

The Discussion is more difficult to correct than the Results. In the latter case, I need only cross out everything that isn't a fact or observation. But the Discussion is more involved. Dissecting it is akin to disentangling a tumor from healthy tissue: sometimes the borders are very indistinct. A statement such as, "The sodium bicarbonate in the test tube provided the plant with a source of carbon," is okay; but "It was fascinating to see the sodium bicarbonate giving carbon to the plant" is not, because the process cannot be directly observed (and, needless to say, "fascinating" tells me nothing). To the student, however, such a differentiation may seem like splitting hairs. That's why I have them write lab after lab after lab until the writing becomes almost automatic. It's like listening repeatedly to a song—after a while it gets stuck in your head, whether you like it or not.

Of course, even when their writing is not on track, my students have an unconscious (or perhaps conscious) way of making it difficult for me to be cut and dried with my corrections. This happens when they end their Discussions by extolling my virtues as a teacher, usually by appending something like, "Thanks for giving me a great lab experience! I'm going to tell all my friends to take your course." Or something more subtle, such as, "I didn't realize how much I didn't know until I did this amazing experiment [on the crawling behavior of the sea slug]." Now how do I lower the boom on their writing after reading such heartfelt sentiments as these? (The answer: Gently. Very gently.)

Science writing is not like the type of writing done by students in the humanities. This is why it so often steamrolls them. Students who have otherwise fine writing skills often have a terrible time transferring those skills to the sciences. In a way, these students are the most difficult to deal with, because they have high opinions of the quality of their work and have achieved good grades on the writing assignments they have done in other courses. It is difficult to convey the message that yes, they can write well, but science writing is about structure, format, and dispassion. Even James Watson and Francis Crick's 1953 paper on the structure of DNA, one of the seminal scientific discoveries of the twentieth century, began with the less-than-rousing, "We wish to suggest a structure for the salt of deoxyribose nucleic acid (D.N.A.). This structure has novel features that are of considerable biological interest." (Of course, if Watson and Crick had been in my class I would have circled "interest" and suggested a rewrite.)

In the end, I suppose, writing is writing in the sense that students suffer from the same unifying malady no matter what they are asked to draft—the lack of willingness to rewrite. I can usually get them to "edit down" and cross out unnecessary language, but when I suggest that a paragraph or—gasp—entire assignment be revisited and overhauled, the looks they give me bespeak horror, or the sense that I have judged their lives as somehow unworthy. By way of compromise, they sometimes take a "death of a thousand cuts" approach to revision, coming to my office again and again with their papers in which they have inserted a missing comma, corrected some misspellings, or indented the first line of their paragraphs in the hope of elevating their grade, however marginally. When I suggested to one student that he edit out angry language (his sow bug would not retreat from the light, and this, in his words, "ticked me off"), he paused, looked down at his paper and then up at me and asked, "If I do, will I get another point?"

But it's important, to say the least, to remember and emphasize the role of encouragement. When I correct a student's lab report, I strive to begin with something positive. "This structure is exactly what I'm looking for." "You've presented your data clearly and carefully." "I couldn't have written this Purpose better myself." I have found that such affirmation at the outset softens the blow of the sometimes-brisk criticism to follow. The students cling to such opening, considerate comments as evidence that, even if their Results and Discussion don't quite make the grade (yet), they are indeed capable of good work, which of course most of them are. And in those instances where their writing falls short, they can always tell me that I'm the greatest teacher since Plato. And hope for the best. ✤

i, teacher

✼ ✼ ✼ ✼ ✼ ✼ ✼ ✼ ✼ ✼ ✼ ✼ ✼ ✼ ✼ ✼ ✼
i rock

As a college professor, I am responsible for grading my students at the end of the semester. What is less well known to those outside the academy is that my students also have an opportunity to grade me.

The grades handed out by the professor don't explain anything: they're just the cold calculus of A, B, C, D, or — gulp — F. (For a while, at my school, a failing grade was represented by an E because, I presume, a student might have been traumatized by an F.) But at the end of the semester, the students themselves get to fill out an extensive anonymous report, rating everything from the professor's expertise to his punctuality to his level of sympathy. At the bottom of this evaluation form, there is a little box where the student can pen a brief statement about the prof, which they have the option of signing.

The whole affair has its own protocol. I cannot be in the classroom while my students are filling out these evals. I hand out the forms, as well as the pencils for filling in the little bubbles, and then select a student to collect the paperwork while I step outside and wonder how I will come out of it this time. Finally, that supervising student emerges and walks past me to deliver the sealed envelope to a secretary for transmittal to the higher ups. Then I return to the classroom and commence my lecture, as if nothing had happened. Now and then a student will catch my eye and give me a thumbs up, although one young man once squinted at me and slowly shook his head.

I have met teachers who are apprehensive about these student evaluations. One colleague was despondent because a student had filled in the "Not at all" bubble for the statement, "Teacher shows concern about student progress." Another had received a "Not at all" from nearly half his class for the statement, "Instructor demonstrates knowledge of material." "But I have a Ph.D.!" he exclaimed while standing in my office with his hands in his hair. (My inclination was to remark, "So much for Ph.D.s"; but what I wound up saying was, "There, there.")

Another colleague—with whom I had only fleeting interactions—was said to have collected the evals himself from his unwitting students (I can picture him saying to his class, in his clipped manner, "Don't worry about these. I'll take care of them.") Then he'd take them to his austere office, draw the shade, and commence the editing process. In this manner, a professor thought to be mediocre at best wound up with student evaluations that consistently placed him slightly lower than the angels.

I suppose I have been fortunate when it comes to these evaluations. For one thing, I tend to forget about them until the end of the semester, when the secretary begins to hector me about deadlines, the result being that I don't teach with these evals in mind, which is good: when the desire for approbation becomes the driving force in a teacher's performance, the course in general can get a little soggy as the prof attempts to avoid the shoal waters of student disapproval by attenuating grades or making extraordinary allowances for students who missed a test because they had a tanning appointment.

For another thing, I have, truth to tell, generally fared well in the eyes of my students, even those who have received poor grades from me. One young man, who failed my introductory biology course, actually wrote in the little space at the bottom of the eval, "Professor Klose was my only friend."

I don't consider myself a vain person, but it is difficult not to feel good about oneself as a teacher and a human being when one's students say nice things about you. After the evaluations have been collected, we faculty receive the data for our review and edification before it is entered into our personnel files. It is a minor moment of truth. There have been semesters when I felt that I had shone as a teacher, and I am gratified when my students pick up on this and evaluate me accordingly. But one cannot please all the people all the time. I recall one enigmatic student who wrote, "Course was too hard, textbook difficult to read, and teacher not very effective." That student had received an A.

For some students, the evaluation form must be too constraining of their sentiments, because on occasion I have found comments written about me in non-traditional places. Most of these estimations have been positive. On one desktop (I sometimes cruise the desktops after my lectures) a student had scribbled, "Klose is the man." What a generous thing to say. And on the cover of a notebook left behind after class, a student had written (in calligraphy) — "Klose rocks." (I immediately took this notebook home to show to my teenage son, who stared at it, uncomprehending, because he was convinced that my biggest problem was that I didn't rock.) Another student had actually engraved a comment into the wooden arm of one of the easy chairs in the student lounge: "Klose is the best psychology teacher on campus." A heartfelt sentiment, the only problem being that I don't teach psychology. (I hope that student eventually found the right class.) And in a men's room stall someone had scrawled — in indelible black ink — "Klose is the best teacher I've ever had. I will miss him." I was humbled by that statement, in particular because it was only the first day of the semester.

I wouldn't be honest if I didn't admit that not all of my evals have been glowing. Recently, for example, I had a young married couple in a very low-level biology course. They were rude and rarely came to class, preferring instead to beg notes from the other students. One day they walked in on the middle of a lecture on the various breeds of dogs. As the students told me about their pets, I explained what they had been bred for. "The dachshund was bred for going down the holes of badgers and rabbits," I said, "which accounts for its elongated shape." "Dalmatians were bred to run with horses; great danes to hunt wild boar."

The woman interjected, "I bet you can't tell me what kind of dog we have."

"A pit bull?" I suggested.

She registered surprise. "How did you guess?"

I went on to explain, "Pit bulls were developed for bringing down bulls that got out of line or behaved wildly on the way to market. This required both strength and aggression."

"But Hans is the gentlest creature in the world!" the husband protested.

"Perhaps he is," I said. "But this variety of dog was not bred for gentleness."

Well, I couldn't mollify either this student or his wife. They both began to grumble. When I got my teacher evals after semester's end, the two of them had written short essays about my lack of professionalism, the woman adding, "He made fun of my dog."

Despite my affection for my students, and my respect for

their efforts to learn biology from me, I have to admit that I have never really been a fan of student evaluations. They have always seemed to me to be a sop thrown to students to lead them to believe that they were having some influence over the quality of their teachers or, more concretely, the status of their employment. The truth is that they probably do neither. Poor teachers receive poor evals, and they continue to teach poorly. The school really has little to lose by maintaining the status quo, because the class that gave the professor the poor evals is soon history, and the next group of students copes with the mediocrity and then achieves the faux catharsis of writing teacher evals at the end of their semester. In short, student evals were not meant to be followed up; they are, simply, evidence that administrative guidelines have been followed.

I have always felt that if students want to evaluate their professors, they can do so, and should be encouraged to. At any point in the semester students can sit down and write either a signed or anonymous letter to the dean, applauding or disapproving of a professor. Such would be an evaluation worth a bit of salt, because it would be initiated by the students themselves, presumably motivated by strong feelings. But alas, this is just a thought; the standard form evals are here to stay, however pro forma they may be.

As I said, I don't consider myself a vain person. Students, and their evaluations, come and go, but I persist. I do my best as a teacher, and I love the work. That's reward enough. But in the interest of making a full breast of things, I have to admit to one instance of self-indulgence.

Several years ago I ran into a former student of mine who had transferred up the road to the University of Maine. She thanked me for having prepared her well, told me of her subsequent successes, and then, almost in afterthought, related how she had been making a phone call in an old-style wooden phone booth in the library. "I dropped my coins," she said, "and while I was fishing around for them on the floor I looked up and saw that someone had written something about you on the underside of the memo platform."

"Really?" I asked, feigning only shallow interest.

"Oh, yes," she assured me, and, to my frustration, left it at that.

I felt foolish, but I couldn't get this out of my mind for several days. I finally decided to give in to my curiosity. I drove up to the university, located the phone booth in question, entered it and, being six-foot-three, had to contort myself to get down on the floor and wedge my head under the memo platform. And then, as I twisted about and squinted in the dim light, I saw it, barely legible, in faint pencil: "Professor Klose is . . ."

"Excuse me."

I glanced up. A young male student was impatiently waiting to use the phone. "Are you done in there?" he asked.

Embarrassed, I groaned to my feet and left the booth. "Dropped a quarter," I said as I exited.

I'm presently working up the courage to go back to find the rest of that inscription.

Just curious, that's all. ⚘

⚘ ⚘ ⚘ ⚘ ⚘ ⚘ ⚘ ⚘ ⚘ ⚘ ⚘ ⚘ ⚘ ⚘ ⚘ ⚘ ⚘
the nutty professor

What has become of the eccentrics in the ranks of our professors? From time to time, when I run into a colleague from another institution, I ask if he or she knows of any such individuals. Almost always, the answer is either "no," or a lengthy pause of consideration before offering up a bland example of an octogenarian who drives a motor scooter.

It is often said that higher academia is not the "real world."

I'm not so sure how true this is today, what with the distinction between gutter and campus highly blurred, and practical emphases on job placement and technological "know how" supplanting the liberal arts. But looking back at my undergraduate years in the 1970s, I do think I studied in a sort of bubble highlighted by, for lack of a better descriptor, wacky professors who may not have been able to function outside the ivory tower.

I recently unearthed one of my college notebooks. On the inside back cover I had caricatured each of my instructors from that particular year. One glance and I immediately recalled the inspirations for my artwork.

There was, for example, Professor Feigenblatt, who walked with a stiff limp and chain-smoked during his German lectures. After each smoke he would drop the still-glowing butt onto the carpet and slowly grind it in with the tip of his orthopedic shoe. As a preamble to every lecture, he would clop over to the desk of each of the Fräuleins present and would ask permission to remove his sports jacket. Then he would light up and begin his rambling lectures while blowing smoke in our faces. On one occasion when he was absent, he sent his elderly German secretary —replete with bifocals on a pearl chain and her hair in a bun— to proctor a test we were taking. I approached her desk with a question from that test. To my surprise, and delight, she gave me the answer, loud enough for everyone to hear. A line quickly formed at her desk, and she dutifully helped all of us out. "Ach," she said, giggling, "if Professor Feigenblatt ever finds out he'll be so annoyed." We all promised we wouldn't tell. The professor returned the following week with the tests in hand, his face aglow. "Wonderful grades!" he exulted. "Everybody got an A!"

Professor Gleason was a bumbling biologist whom, due to his generous and ovoid physical proportions, we students had nicknamed "The Egg." He seemed to be totally baffled by his own course material, and managed quite capably to convey this bewilderment to the class, so that none of us knew what the hell was going on. I once went to his office with great trepidation to ask him to explain a challenging concept. When I arrived there he had his back to me as he stood before an elaborate apparatus of glassware, ringstands, tubes, and clamps. I recall thinking, Well, how about that? Still waters run deep. He does know what he's doing after all. When he turned to me, however, he was stirring a cup of coffee, brewed on the intricate set-up. One day he took us down to the banks of the Hackensack River for a field trip. We helped him get the large motorboat into the water, and then the ten of us students looked on from the bank as he worked away at the engine, yanking the pull repeatedly to get it to start. He hadn't noticed that the boat had begun to drift away, and we had no intention of alerting him. We all watched in silence (and with rising anticipation of a canceled class) as The Egg worked at the engine, his crablike arms too short to extract the pull all the way. Within ten minutes he had drifted out of sight. So we went home.

My organic chemistry professor, Dr. Weinstein, was rather fearsome and had little patience with students. His reputation didn't rest upon his teaching prowess, because he had only one mantra—"Read the book!" Word was that he had fathered a famous chemical reaction during World War II and continued to get mileage out of that one, shining achievement. He was also as near-sighted as Mr. Magoo. On the first day of class he distributed our glassware and warned us, in his harsh, croaking voice: "I will inventory the glassware at the end of the course. If any is missing, you'll pay!"

Well, there was inevitable breakage during the semester, and a lot of it. On the last day, Weinstein told us to stand shoulder-to-shoulder in front of the lab benches while he walked from student to student with his clipboard. For our part, we were passing the glassware to one another behind our backs in such a way that everyone wound up with a "complete" set. "Well," rasped Weinstein when he was done inventorying. "That's a first." If he later discovered the deficits, it didn't matter, because his eyesight was so bad that he would never be able to identify any of us.

Professor Miriam Holzer taught an elective in sociology. In addition to her atrocious hats, one of which resembled the bread fungus *Rhizopus*, her most salient gloss was her inability to find not only our classroom, but the campus as well. It was Professor Holzer's first semester at the university, and we took full advantage of her complete mystification about the location of the campus. After missing the first class and arriving thirty minutes late for the second, she turned to us and asked for the best way to get from her home to the school. We told her to proceed in a completely contrary direction, up the Taconic State Parkway. She did so, and missed the next class. But when she surfaced again she seemed not the least bit more witting about what had happened and asked us for directions again! This time we sent her to Queens. Eventually she discovered the correct route to the school. I would like to say that she forgave us for the shenanigans; but why would she? She never suspected we were taking advantage of her.

Mrs. Reynard (she was an instructor and not a titled professor) taught English lit. Her specialty was Romantic English poetry. The thing was, she couldn't remember who had written what. One day she commenced a rolling commentary on Robert Browning, beginning with his biography and then dissecting his metrical technique with the focus and deliberation of a brain surgeon. She ended her discourse with the comment, "Once you've read Browning, you'll never forget him." Then she recited a poem, "The Birth of Love," after which she placed her hand on her heart and sighed. A student spoke up. "But Mrs. Reynard," he said, "that's Wordsworth." "Oh," she said, and blinked uncomprehendingly as she began to page through the text in search of Browning.

Professor O'Rourke, of psychology, was the epitome of the absent-minded professor. He was the type who pushed his glasses up on his head and then spent the next fifteen minutes looking for them. He could often be seen wandering around the parking lot searching for his car before realizing that he'd taken the bus.

He once went into the men's room with his briefcase and came out with the toilet seat under his arm. I kid you not. But within his discipline he was absolutely crackerjack.

In the jaded eyes of us students, it was clear that our professors would have a hard time functioning in the wider world. Gleason, we knew, would never be a boat pilot, O'Rourke would fail miserably as a parking valet, and Holzer's inability to connect points A and B would automatically disqualify her from driving a cab.

But I miss these people. Or better said, I lament not having colleagues like them in my teaching environment. Where have the outlandish characters gone? My sense is that the nature of the university beast has changed and has had a leveling effect on the spectrum of personalities. As higher education has striven to define itself as a business ("Students are our customers!" chirps a perky poster), there is less tolerance for professors who might — heaven forbid — embarrass the institution and drive the paying public away. The result has been a more rigid screening of applicants for conformity, or, in the lingo of current hiring practices, "institutional fit." This is a catch-all phrase that colleges and universities use to trump all other qualifications and acquire the person they had their eye on all along. In other words, a brilliant eccentric who can simultaneously write Greek with one hand and Latin with the other while captivating his students has less institutional fit than a bland monotone who sticks to the text and is grateful to the administration for giving him a job.

What about me? I don't think I'm eccentric, or cranky, or absent-minded. What professors with these characteristics have in common is their unwittingness: the prof is out of touch, to a greater or lesser degree, with his surroundings and especially with how his students regard him. I still recall an event at the end of Professor Gleason's biology class. Between semesters we had a seven-week break. At the beginning of the break a few of us went to his office and put a few fruit flies in his desk drawer along with enough food to sustain several generations. When we returned to school after our lengthy vacation we followed The Egg across campus as he waddled toward his building. We waited outside his office as he arranged his things, got his coffee apparatus going again, and then, as he opened his drawer, screamed out, "Oh, my God!" This was followed by a frantic racket as he swatted at the swarm with what sounded like a frying pan. But he apparently never suspected a thing. He certainly didn't interrogate any of us. The cozy academic life for him simply went on.

Now, if I were to open my desk drawer one morning and recoil as thousands of fruit flies streamed out, I'd immediately know something was up, and I'd immediately suspect my students. Then I would plan my counterattack. Perhaps this comes from having grown up in rough and tumble New Jersey, where interpersonal warfare is part of the social fabric and nobody is allowed to get away with anything.

I was recently at a gathering of colleagues, some of whom had brought their college-age children along. I took the opportunity to ask if any of them knew any true eccentrics at their schools. Those of my generation (baby boom) and older had colorful stories to tell from their undergraduate days. But not one of the kids could describe a prof who was outrageous or singular in any but the most benign and modest of ways. Their teachers were, for the most part, unmemorable.

Oh, where have they gone? Where are these helpless, hopeless, unaware yet frequently gifted personalities who, like planets orbiting their stars, never stray far from the schools that give them comfort and purpose? Is there nowhere to be found a philosophy professor who has taught his mynah bird to recite the odes of Pindar? Or a physicist in search of a perpetual motion machine? Perhaps a linguist who is working on toe sign language? Our eccentrics and dreamers and mental drifters have been replaced with pragmaticians who have mapped their courses out with all the precision and predictability of masons building a wall. Nothing is left to the imagination, and even their attempts at humor abrade us specifically because we know they are trying to be funny for our sakes. How much more wonderful it is when a professor makes us laugh because his world is odd, his steps sometimes unsure, his glasses eternally lost upon his head, the toilet seat propped under his arm.

I have heard it said that nostalgia is a form of protest. And I suppose it is, because I feel a longing for something I once had and that I now miss. I realize that one cannot hire a new professor because he or she is eccentric, but what's sad is that hiring committees no longer overlook eccentricity in their constant striving for institutional fit. Perhaps this is because eccentricity has become conflated with liability. The only hope, then, in the current social climate, is for eccentricity to rise to the level of a disability that would have to be accommodated. Then these colorful people would have a fighting chance and colleges and universities would be presented with opportunities to become more interesting places again. ✲

✲ ✲ ✲ ✲ ✲ ✲ ✲ ✲ ✲ ✲ ✲ ✲ ✲ ✲ ✲ ✲ ✲

a seat at the periodic table

Introductory biology texts traditionally begin with basic chemistry and from there move on to the cell and then to whole organisms, ending with ecology and evolution. There is some logic in this small-to-big approach, this crescendo of themes.

I take a different tack. I begin with a discussion of evolution (the big picture), because I believe that students need a context in which to couch the rest of the course information. Only after I have dealt with Darwin—and after it's too late for my students to drop the course without penalty—do I take up the gauntlet of chemistry, an area my non-majors generally dread as a result of bad high school experiences or assumptions about its difficulty.

Truth to tell, I love teaching the chemistry section. Compared to the ifs, ands or buts of biology (nerves cannot regenerate, except in certain instances when . . .), chemistry is constant, symmetrical, and mechanical. If you can build a tiny helium atom, then you can use the exact same building blocks to construct an outsized uranium atom. Just like Legos.

Why is it important to teach chemistry at all in a biology course? Because many biological processes are understandable only in terms of chemistry: molecular genetics, photosynthesis, the transmission of nerve impulses, immunology, diffusion, osmosis, and on and on. Chemistry, in short, is a plinth supporting the soaring column of biology (or, to appropriate Frost, biology is a "pinnacle to heavenward / [that] signifies the sureness of the soul," thanks to the reliability and consistency of chemical laws).

But chemistry, in turn, has its own cornerstone—a systematic list or chart of the pure substances that make up not only the earth, but, so far as we know, the rest of the universe as well. This list or chart is called the Periodic Table of the Elements. If chemistry were a republic conceived in logic and dedicated to the proposition that everything in the universe is made up of the same "stuff," then the periodic table would be kept in a glass chamber filled with nitrogen (element #7) for all its citizens to revere.

Alas, science is more detached and dispassionate than this, and, in a biology course at least, the periodic table seldom receives the emphasis and accolades it deserves. I spend an entire lecture on it. When I first project an image of the periodic table of the elements for my students, there is a low, collective groan of discontent when they behold all those symbols and numbers. Before I can get a word out of my mouth, someone, usually a smart aleck in the back row, speaking for the entire class, preempts me with, "Do we have to know all of those?" (There are over one hundred elements.) And even before I can say, "No, but . . ." there is a follow-up groan, as if they were Vikings being ordered to row faster. "Jeesh," I lament. "Give me a break." And then I lapse into one of my New Jersey stories, which soothes their discontent.

When I was a kid I had my own laboratory in the basement of my family's Jersey City home. I whiled away many hours in that dark recess, mostly mixing rocket fuel from the saltpeter (potassium nitrate) I had wheedled out of Patsy, the local butcher, so I could launch an ant into "space." I also read a great deal of chemistry. I didn't understand many of its quantitative aspects, but I had a good head for the descriptive parts and I knew how to work equations. I was also taken with the biographies of the great historical chemists — Paracelsus, Humphrey Davy, Joseph Priestley (who never took a science course but went on anyway to discover carbon dioxide and, by extension, soda pop), and, arguably, the greatest historical name in all of chemistry, Dmitri Mendeleev, a nineteenth-century Russian.

I emphasize Mendeleev for two reasons. One is that he personified the often-underestimated value of single-mindedness (he told his long-suffering wife that his true bride was science); two is that he looked at the sixty-three elements then known and recognized that they were not a random jumble of substances but could instead be logically ordered according to their properties and their atomic weights.

When I say that Mendeleev ordered the elements, I mean that he is credited with laying out the modern periodic table. The thing about Mendeleev is that he had a romantic view of science, which he conflated with art and love. And being a Russian, his mind was guided by a sense of fatalism. In this spirit, perhaps, he developed a passion for the elements and was convinced that they could be arranged in some logical scheme. He didn't do a single experiment to work this out, but is said to have instead written the elements' symbols down on blank cards (each element has a chemical symbol; for example, H = hydrogen, O = oxygen, Hg = mercury. Why Hg? Please stand by) along with their chemical characteristics and began a long, repetitive game of solitaire. What he discovered, in short, is that every so often he'd "play" a card containing an element that had properties similar to a card that had been played earlier. He then rearranged the cards so that similar elements were in the same row. This is what is known as "periodicity," hence the *Periodic* Table of the Elements.

The discovery of periodicity, however, was only one coup. The next had a whiff of mysticism about it: every so often Mendeleev found that he didn't have an element card for the next play. It was as if the element simply didn't exist. And now for the genius part: he played a blank card; but by studying the other, known elements in the same group, he was able to *predict* the properties of not-yet-discovered elements and exactly where they would fit into the blank spots in his table once they were identified. When he suggested this, it didn't, at first, elicit much interest among his peers. But as the years peeled away, one-by-one these new elements were indeed discovered, and they fit perfectly into the vacancies in Mendeleev's burgeoning table, with precisely the properties he had predicted they would have. Mendeleev's reputation widened in tandem with the filling in of the blank spots in his periodic table.

If I tell this story with enough verve, I find that I can hook my students. And then, to cement their interest, another personal note. I tell them how, as a teenager working away in my basement laboratory, Mendeleev's story captivated and inspired me. I too became fascinated with the elements and began my own collection. I already knew that I would not bother with the gases, whose invisibility makes them no fun to look at, or with the radioactive elements, for fear of waking up with extra toes or fathering freaks. But the other elements were fair game, and many were very easy to come by. I got iron (symbol Fe) filings by (what else?) filing iron. I already had sulfur (S) from my rocket fuel experiments. Carbon (C) came from the aquarium filter. I asked my dentist for mercury (the pesky Hg again) and he took a squeeze bottle and kindly squirted some into my hand (these were the pre-EPA days) for me to carry home. One night I was watching a *Star Trek* episode, the one with Horta the silicon (Si) beast, who could write (but not speak) English ("No kill I!"). So I wrote to U.S. Steel and they sent me a few vials of silicon. I soon had an enviable collection.

I relate these stories about my element collection and about Mendeleev to my students because I think it's important that they know how their crazy professor got his start in science and who his heroes are, and also that science does not precipitate out of thin air but is the result of dogged labor by real people. Then I do a show-and-tell with my elements, one-by-one, holding them up in their little vials as I describe their properties with something like love in my eyes. There's stark yellow sulfur, from the deep recesses of the earth; a coil of magnesium (Mg), a metal that burns with a blinding white flame; and the gold (Au) from my failed dental crown. I also have some exotics on hand: vanadium (V), a lovely metal named after Vanadis, the Scandinavian goddess of beauty; bromine (Br), the only liquid element that's not a metal; and gallium (Ga), a soft metal that would melt in the heat of your mouth but not the cool of your hand, like an M&M.

Mercury is always a hit with my students, because it's a metal one can play with. When you shake the vial it wiggles, breaks up into smaller globules, and then reunites into a seamless puddle. These qualities inspired mercury's early, common name, quicksilver — in archaic English, "quick" means living, as in "the quick and the dead." In other words, it was once thought that mercury was a living metal. Now I can tell you why its chemical symbol is Hg. Many elements that were known early on have Latin or Greek symbols, such as Sn for tin (Latin: stannum), Ag for silver (argentum), and, my favorite, Pb for lead (plumbum, hence plumbing). In the case of mercury, Hg is from the Greek "hydragyrum," which means "liquid silver." Science, you see, is heaven for language enthusiasts.

What good is having a collection if you can't share it with

others? After my spiel, I pass my elements around with the admonition, "Please don't open the containers!" It's good advice, because many elements are quite toxic and others are very reactive when exposed to air/moisture. This is especially true of the so-called "alkali metals" like sodium (Na), potassium (K) and calcium (Ca). If these make contact with water they will explode. In fact, while some very stable elements, like gold, platinum, and helium, are found freely in nature, most elements do not exist naturally in their pure states precisely because they are so reactive. Consider the Statue of Liberty: when new she looked like a bright, shiny penny; but she oxidized (her copper combined with oxygen) over time, which is a good thing, because the greenish "patina" of copper oxide is what protects the elemental copper beneath from further degradation.

In order to drive home this important point—that there's a good reason most elements are not lying around in the open air—I tell the tale of a truly important, common, and reactive element: sodium.

When I was fourteen I read about sodium's touchy nature in a Funk & Wagnall's encyclopedia and resolved to get my hands on some as quickly as possible. Living in New Jersey, I had ready access to chemical plants. (Just down the street from me was a factory that made detonators for nuclear weapons—they would often test these devices at night. Once, when I was five years old, I woke up crying and my father came into my bedroom to comfort me. "Don't worry," he said. "They're only testing parts for atomic bombs.") One day, on a lark, I called one of these companies and asked if they had any sodium. "Yes," the kind man said. "We do. It's $4.64 a pound." Barely able to contain myself, I placed my order and, when my father came home for lunch, asked him for a lift. My dad was a salesman who knew nothing about chemistry, but he was big on education and always willing to help me out. So off we went.

It's hard for me to describe my elation upon visiting a real chemical factory. Just to smell the heavy, acrid air, walk among the stacked barrels of reagents, and see flaming towers of waste gas was an incomparable thrill. I picked up the sodium (or, rather, had my father make the transaction) and, once back in my basement laboratory, I carved off a piece about the size of a walnut (sodium is a very soft metal). Then I led about eight of my friends down the street and chucked it into Mrs. Topchevski's swimming pool. It bubbled and smoked and then — bang! Up it went in a brilliant yellow flame.

This story greatly excites my students. What they don't know is that I am still a patron of the sodium market and keep a small supply on hand. So, after whipping them up to fever pitch with my story, I take them outside and direct them to stand at a safe distance while I drop a chunk of sodium into a coffee can of water and run. Seconds later — bang! — a yellow flash and a smoke ring, and my students are converts. The only things missing are the "Hallelujahs."

I perform this experiment not to relive the glories of my wayward childhood, but to deliver the important lesson about why most elements do not exist in their free states in nature. Sodium is an extreme example of why it can't be found lying around (if it did exist in its pure state, think what would happen when it rained). Less reactive elements like copper, iron, and aluminum would simply oxidize and quietly waste away. Most elements are therefore found only in combination with other elements to form compounds. Such alliances radically change the elements' properties. Take sodium chloride — table salt — for example. Sodium is an explosive metal, chlorine a choking, toxic gas; but when you combine them you get a white crystal you can sprinkle on your hamburger. Compounds are nature's way of giving elements safe havens, but the price of this stability is that they lose their reactivity.

Because of Mendeleev, we can look at a periodic table and get a sense of the properties of each of the elements simply by being familiar with some of their neighbors. Sodium is very unstable; therefore potassium, calcium, and strontium, which are in the same family, must also be unstable. Helium is highly stable and will not combine with any other elements (that is, there is no such thing as helium chloride); therefore the other elements in its group — argon, krypton, and xenon — will also not combine. (These elements are what are known as the inert or noble gases: they're snobs who want nothing to do with other elements.)

When I finish my three-lecture section on chemistry, I always feel that I am saying goodbye to a friend. Maybe this is because chemistry is so wrapped up in my nostalgia for the experiments I survived when I was a kid. But I also don't like taking leave of Mendeleev, who became a real superhero in his time (except to the tsarist government, which didn't approve of his republican leanings) and embodied the highest standards of science in his belief that through patient, focused probing of the data, answers will inevitably reveal themselves.

In addition to sodium's pyrotechnic lesson, I hope my students carry this one home as well. ✦

atoms in love

The non-science-majors' fear of science is legendary. When cornered into taking a science course, they invariably select biology, the "non-math" science. In my experience, rarely does anyone elect to take chemistry for the fun of it. And with good reason. Chemistry is perceived as complicated, abstract, and quantitative. The triple whammy.

In my introductory biology course I cover chemistry for a little over a week. I have to. Many biological processes cannot be understood without at least a passing familiarity with the molecules that make them go. How can one talk about digestion without mentioning enzymes without mentioning enzymatic structure without mentioning how enzymes function? Actually, there are practitioners of the art of science teaching who say that this is indeed possible, through the development of courses with condescending names like "Biology for Poets." This is not far removed from "Biology for Idiots," which should be the purview of the mass-market paperback industry and not the universities.

Be that as it may, and despite my bravado and calls for purism, I often find myself succumbing to the allure of creative imagery, romantic notions, and fantastic story lines to clarify concepts that my students struggle with.

Take atoms, for example. These particles form the smallest part of any element. You can have an atom of gold, oxygen, boron, einsteinium, or any other element, but not less than this. If two or more atoms bump into one another they may combine to form a molecule. For example, H_2O is a molecule consisting of two atoms of hydrogen and one atom of oxygen. The question is, how does this happen? And there lies the rub. In order to understand how atoms combine, or bond, we have to look inside them.

All atoms consist of smaller units called subatomic particles, of which there are three types: protons, neutrons, and electrons. Atoms work the way they do because they are electrically charged. Protons are positive (think "P for positive"), neutrons neutral ("N for neutral"), and electrons negative (because that's the only charge that's left). Protons and neutrons are nestled together in the central core of the atom, the nucleus. Electrons, for their part, revolve around the nucleus. Picture the solar system: the sun (nucleus) is orbited by planets (electrons).

So far so good (right?). Now, when atoms bond, you can forget about the protons and neutrons. The only thing that matters are the electrons. The question being begged is, how does one know how many electrons an atom has? This is what the Periodic Table of the Elements is for. It's a reference that tells us precisely how many subatomic particles are in the atom of any element. Check out oxygen, symbol O. If you look at the periodic table, oxygen has two numbers associated with it. The smaller number tells us the number of electrons (actually, it tells us the number of protons, but the number of negative charges always equals the number of positive ones, for the sake of balance). In the case of oxygen, this number is eight. My students accept and understand this, and at this point in the lecture everyone is convivial and self-congratulatory.

Now comes a marginally arithmetical step. The electrons occupy distinct regions, or shells, which are at varying distances from the nucleus (picture, again, the concentric orbits of the planets about the sun). The first shell (mercury's orbit) can hold only two electrons. If, as with oxygen, you have more than two electrons, then the "spillover" goes to the next shell (Venus's orbit). So in the case of oxygen, its first shell holds two electrons and its remaining six electrons spill over into the second shell, so that an oxygen atom (ignoring its protons and neutrons) looks something like this:

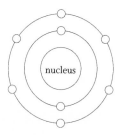

The thing is, every shell beyond the first one can hold a maximum of eight electrons. If the outer shell of any atom has less than its maximum number of electrons, it is, to a greater or lesser degree, unstable, and goes hunting for electrons from other atoms to complete its outer shell. Oxygen's second shell is "missing" two electrons. Place it in a bottle with some hydrogen, apply a spark, and poof! — two hydrogen atoms come in to help oxygen out by donating electrons to complete its outer shell, and water (H_2O) is born.

I enjoy teaching atomic bonding, though the experience be bittersweet because 21.62 percent of the students will not "get" it. While I am describing the process, everyone dutifully nods as if I am quoting scripture. Yet I can look into the eyes of a fifth of the class and see that nobody is home. So I go beyond saying, "Are there any questions?" and tell them outright, "Twenty percent of you don't understand this. Please tell me where the confusion is."

This often does the trick. A couple of hands make tentative stabs at the air. So I move to an analogy. "Let's say you have a series of shelves," I tell them, "one on top of the other. The top shelf is very small and can hold only two cans of peas, but every other shelf below it can hold a maximum of eight. So I give you ten cans of peas and tell you to fill the shelves, starting with the top one." This illustration eases the pain for many, but what hovers in the air between us is the assumption that it can't be this easy. Chemistry is supposed to be *hard*.

After breaking a sweat getting the distribution of electrons right, the truly heavy lifting comes when atoms must be bonded together. I can already feel myself slipping away into the realm of fantasy, knowing, intellectually, that I may be misleading my students with romantic analogies, yet hoping that they will eventually forget my antics and, in the end, have a clear idea of what actually happens when atoms bed down together. "Listen," I begin, once again dealing with oxygen and hydrogen. "Oxygen has only six electrons in its outer shell. This means it needs two electrons, and each of the two hydrogen atoms has an electron to share. It's a match made in heaven. Oxygen and hydrogen *want* to be together. It will fulfill all their desires for stability."

Oy! If a real chemist could hear me he'd think I had lost my mind. But oxygen *is* particularly loose with its morals. It will bond, promiscuously, with almost anything. The products of this sleeping around are substances called "oxides." Copper oxide, iron oxide, nickel oxide, aluminum oxide, etc. Leave your bike out in the rain and oxygen will seduce it to rust. Enjoy a shiny new copper penny while you have it, because before long oxygen will have carnal, oxidizing knowledge of it, turning it brown.

When the limits of my students' comprehension are pressed even further, I engage in ever more far-flung descriptions to make my point. "Carbon has been looking for hydrogen all its life, and at last has found fulfillment as methane (CH_4)." "Helium is a committed bachelor. It has only one shell and this shell already has its maximum allotment of two electrons. Helium doesn't need anybody else. It is a lonely atom."

Love. Loneliness. Longing. Unprotected sex. Sometimes I wonder whether I am elucidating or confounding the issue. All I can say in my own defense is that the impulse to make these concepts compelling to the point of understanding is strong, and it is this impulse that propels me into the buffer between hard-nosed scientific facts and the dream world of the Harlequin romance.

The only thing that occasionally gives me pause is the sight of my students taking all of this down as I speak. What on earth can they be writing with such gusto? One day I had the opportunity to find out, and all because I could not resist temptation. I am a weak man.

After a chemistry lecture in which I described explosive sodium and poisonous chlorine's wild courtship to create tasty salt (sodium chloride), I noticed that a student had left his notebook under his desk. I eyed it for a few long moments, wondering if I should or shouldn't open it to take a peek, knowing that students often write things in their notebooks that have nothing to do with the course and are not meant for other eyes.

I eventually sidled over to the notebook and, after a quick, furtive glance about, began to flip through the pages. As with many of the notebooks I find, there was no name, no way to identify whose it was. I paged to the chemistry lecture and, well, the graphics were about right, but the notes were embellishments upon my embellishments. Here's one entry: "Oxygen is in love with hydrogen. The feeling is mutual. If you put them together in a bedroom and light a candle you'll get water. Oxygen will get together with anybody. It just doesn't care. Oxygen is a slut."

How could I not smile at this student's extrapolations? She (I later found out it was a she) was right. Oxygen is a slut. But it also cares. It's just misunderstood. In actuality, oxygen has its standards—there are elements it will not bond with—and is simply in search of quality companionship. It's just that so often the results of its dalliances are unpleasant to the eye (again, think of rust).

Taking such liberties with chemistry is an indulgence that suits the teaching of non-majors just fine. In fact, I believe it's sometimes the best way to get these concepts across, because there's so little at stake: the exposure to chemistry that I give them will probably be all they ever learn about elements, atoms, and molecules. Clearly, if these were chemistry majors bound for industry or grad school, I'd have to be more orthodox in my approach. Or would I?

When I was an undergrad I was required to take two semesters of organic chemistry, a legendarily challenging course dealing with carbon-based compounds. Although I had a truly fine teacher, I can recall only two specifics from the course: one, that the professor wore a wig; and two, a story he told about the German chemist Friedrich Kekulé, who, in a half-sleep, received a vision of a serpent biting its own tail, which immediately suggested to him the structure of the benzene ring—the precursor molecule of thousands of useful compounds, including drugs, plastics, and dyes.

I can still draw the benzene molecule, because of the snake story. Of course, in my class this would no doubt be transformed into a moral about self-love.

But one has to start somewhere. ⚑

forbidden fruits

✴ ✴ ✴ ✴ ✴ ✴ ✴ ✴ ✴ ✴ ✴ ✴ ✴ ✴ ✴ ✴ ✴

what hath darwin wrought?

Once, while reading the graffiti in a stall in the men's room at my college, I came across the following scrawl: DARWIN WAS WRONG!

I immediately realized that I had inspired this wisdom, as I had just that very morning broached the topic of evolution in my introductory biology course, during which a woman in the back row quietly seethed as I pressed inexorably onward with the incendiary material.

I tried to erase the comment by spitting on my thumb and rubbing it, but the marker was of the indelible type. The symbolism wasn't lost on me: of all the world's nations, the United States is touted as being the most technologically advanced, yet the idea of evolution — accepted without a whimper in even Third World backwaters — is still fodder for controversy here. Like the graffito in that stall, it just won't go away. In 1999, for example — long after the Scopes trial was thought to have been the final catharsis in the battle to "allow" evolution to be taught in American public schools — the Kansas Board of Education voted to "reject evolution as a scientific principle."

It seems trite, at this juncture in the ongoing battle, to ask, "Why should this be?" The answer is no secret: religious fundamentalism. This was encapsulated for me in a very direct and personal way when that seething woman in my class decided to take action. At the conclusion of my lecture, she marched up to me and, with fire in her eyes and a raised, accusing finger, declaimed the following: "For what you have taught today you shall be damned to the everlasting fires of hell."

So.

After a moment's pause, I gave her the only answer that seemed appropriate: "We never learned anything we weren't meant to know."

It helped a little. She took a step back and examined me with a cold eye. "How can you speak so glibly about a theory that's not even true?" she demanded.

A theory? I once saw a cartoon that said it best: Evolution may have started out as a theory, but it evolved into a fact a long time ago. Still, the expression "theory of evolution" is so well grounded that even many scientists unconsciously utter it.

Evolution is not a theory. We know that the earth's environment has been changing constantly since the planet's origin. Maine, for example, was once tropical (during the Cretaceous Period, more than sixty-five million years ago). We also know that, if a species population is to survive, it must, over time, adapt to its ever-changing environment or else it will go the way of the dodo. If Florida were to embark upon a long-term (hundreds or thousands of years) chilling trend, does anyone really believe that palm trees would persist in their present form? Something, in short, would have to give. The heartiest palm trees would have the best chance of surviving the creeping cold, and they would therefore pass their "cold resistance" genes on to their offspring. In time, these palms would change so much that they would become a type of tree—a new species—that could survive the frostier climate that would come to characterize Florida.

What I have just described is the mechanism by which evolution works. It's called Natural Selection, and it is *this* that is the theoretical part of evolution. Natural Selection was the long-suffering, hypochondriacal Charles Darwin's brilliant idea, and virtually all mainstream scientists accept at least its broad assertions.

There are other theories of the fact of evolution as well. Some have been discredited, such as Jean Baptiste LaMarck's eighteenth-century idea of "use and disuse," which states that if an individual "needs" a change in its body, it acquires this change and passes it on to its offspring (that is, if a monkey stretches its arms they will get longer, and the monkey will then have long-armed babies).

Other ideas have complemented or even competed with Darwin's theory of natural selection. An example is the theory of "punctuated equilibrium," postulated by the paleontologist Niles Eldredge and the late evolutionary biologist Stephen Jay Gould, which views much of evolution not as a long, hard crawl (Darwin's idea), but rather the result of natural calamities abruptly altering its course. Gould once wrote that the most probable reason for the extinction of the dinosaurs was a meteoric impact some sixty million years ago. The resulting disappearance of the thunder lizards opened the way for the ascent of the mammals. (In other words, we're lucky to be here. Evolution didn't have to lead to us.)

The woman who described my future career as a raker of coals in Gehenna was not a singular case. At least once a semester I have a student who objects to my teaching evolution. For the most part they are subtle and respectful. On a written exam I once included the following question: "Contrast Darwin's Theory of Natural Selection with LaMarck's Theory of Evolution by Acquired Characteristics." One young man answered the question clearly and completely. But at the end of his answer he wrote, "Turn paper over." I did so, and found an unsolicited addendum, to wit: "I don't believe any of this evolution stuff, but I am giving you the answer you are looking for because I want to do well on this test."

How can one quarrel with such honesty? And yet, this student's grudging cooperation left me somewhat cold. He was, in essence, claiming that I was teaching false information. As one who believes in a world of infinite possibilities (and as a subscriber to Cromwell's famous quote, "I beseech you, in the bowels of Christ, think it possible you may be mistaken"), I freely admit that any of the concepts I teach could turn out to be wrong, in which case I would make the appropriate corrections and updates, and proceed from there. This approach serves the needs of everybody, whereas teaching false information serves only the needs of the promulgator (thus are tyrants born).

In other words, I am a teacher, not a politician.

At the Scopes trial in 1925, William Jennings Bryan, the fundamentalist, three-time Democratic candidate for President of the United States, prosecuted the self-effacing John Scopes, the young man (he was only twenty-three) who had been accused of teaching evolution to his high school biology class in contravention of a Tennessee state law that prohibited the teaching of any theory that contradicted the biblical account of Creation. Opposing Bryan was the most famous defense lawyer of the time, Clarence Darrow (who had, the previous year, by means of a long and impassioned speech, saved the child-killers Leopold and Loeb from certain death sentences). The trial took place in Dayton, Tennessee, which the journalist H. L. Mencken called "this bright, shining, buckle of the Bible belt."

The turning point in the trial—which had been going badly for Scopes—was Darrow's masterstroke of putting the prosecution, Bryan, on the witness stand and exposing his ignorance to his claque of hooting supporters. Specifically, Darrow tripped Bryan up on the question of the age of the earth. Bryan, sweating horribly under Darrow's relentless assault, finally admitted that the lengths of the six days of Creation were open to interpretation. In other words, they were not necessarily twenty-four-hour days. ("My impression is that they were periods," said Bryan.) Darrow immediately pounced. If those days could have been of indeterminate length, then perhaps they were millions of years in duration. For Bryan, it was downhill from there. He won his case (Scopes was fined a nominal $100, later overturned on appeal), but Darrow had humiliated him before his rural fundamentalist base. He died in Dayton two weeks later, from heart failure. (See Mencken's merciless essay, "In Memoriam, W.J.B.," for his take on Bryan's legacy.)

Bryan, as a fundamentalist, believed in a strict, literal reading of the Bible, according to which—if one does some creative math with the ages of the prophets mentioned in Genesis—the earth was created in 4004 B.C. This figure was first posited by a Bishop Usher, of Ireland, in the seventeenth century, who more specifically stated that the first day of Creation began on the evening preceding October 23rd of that year. At the Scopes trial, Bryan appeared not to dispute this date, asserting to Darrow, "that is Bishop Usher's calculation."

Sound ridiculous? Just as there are people who still believe that the earth is flat, there are, living today, tie-dyed fundamentalists who adhere to this scripture-based calculation of the date of Creation with a matter-of-factness so stark that it is difficult to come up with a meaningful response. I came face-to-face with one of these people, a student, a thirtyish man who was having a tremendous struggle in my biology course.

Phil was not stupid. He was reasonably articulate but ignorant, knowing almost nothing about science, history, or literature. But one October day (it was not the twenty-third) I felt the heat of his ire at my back as he sat in class, arms folded across his chest, slowly shaking his head as I detailed what we knew about the age of the earth. When I mentioned that the most recent estimate was about four-and-a-half billion years, he just couldn't take it anymore and attempted to set me straight. "Six thousand years," he declaimed, bringing his right hand down in karate chops upon his desk.

The irony was that he was a member of the local Penobscot tribe of Indians. "Phil," I said, "there were Indians in Maine long before that. These were your own people."

Phil immediately got to his feet and headed for the door. But then, suddenly, he turned and yelled out at me, "Darwin was wrong!" Then he left the building (making one pit stop, perhaps, in the men's room?).

The rest of the class was understandably unnerved by the blow-up. But the event brought something of interest to mind, an insight of sorts. Over the years a number of students have exited the course because they had a problem with evolution. What I was left with was a group of students who were able to accept evolution and incorporate it into their understanding of how the world works. I was, unwittingly, demonstrating natural selection, and here's how: In introducing the topic of evolution, I was causing a change in the teaching environment. Those students who could cope with the change persisted. Those who could not (Phil, for example), were out-competed and "died off." Thus, the ones who were able to adapt to the class had the best chance of surviving to pass on their legacy of scholarship to their offspring.

As I lay in bed one night, this very thought kept needling me. And then, by extrapolation, its analog in the fundamentalist environment hit home: By preaching so vehemently against evolution, fundamentalist organizations are driving from their midst anyone inclined to consider the possibility of such a phenomenon. Eventually, the only people sitting in the pews are those who reject evolution out of hand, and instead cling to a literal reading of scripture. These people would survive to pass on their ignorance to their offspring.

In other words, in trying to run lances through the beast of evolution, the fundamentalists were, instead, demonstrating its central tenet: survival of the fittest.

Once again, the irony.

It is unfortunate that my student objectors to evolution refuse to read anything about it, or otherwise learn what it proposes. Especially since the mere consideration of other ideas does not require that they give up anything besides intransigence. The problem, of course, is that they've confused evolution with Creation. Evolution does not seek to answer the question of why life exists on earth. Darwin himself, writing in the very last paragraph of *The Origin of Species*, his masterpiece, attributes life's origins to "the Creator." How did life get here in the first place? I have no idea. Even science doesn't know, although it has its theories, of course; but observations are impossible, because the event is mired in the remotest days of the planet's past.

However, where facts and theories fail me, imagination thrives. I have no problem anticipating the day when we will understand how life takes root in lifeless places. As of this writing, some three hundred so-called "extrasolar" planets have been discovered—worlds revolving around distant stars. The first ones were gas giants, like Jupiter and Saturn. Then came extrasolar rocky planets; but these were too close to their suns to permit life. The latest additions are rocky planets at Goldilocks distances from their stars—not too hot and not too cold, but just right. And now they've found one of these earthlike planets that seems to have water.

Slowly, but surely, we draw closer. ♠

✼ ✼ ✼ ✼ ✼ ✼ ✼ ✼ ✼ ✼ ✼ ✼ ✼ ✼ ✼ ✼ ✼ ✼
scriptural

There are biology students who don't limit their objections to the teaching of evolution. Sometimes they reject the whole kit and caboodle of science.

Such was the case with Twyla. At first she seemed absolutely unremarkable, sitting in the back of the room, in the corner, reasonably attentive. In fact, the ensuing week was also as placid as a lake in summer, with all of my students, including Twyla, quietly writing in their notebooks as I lectured.

Soon thereafter, I gave the first quiz, in which I asked the students to write down the names of five biology subfields of their choosing and then describe their subject matter. Acceptable answers would have included areas like pathology, the study of disease processes, or mycology, the study of fungi. Twyla did just fine.

But once I got into the more conceptual aspects of biology, such as evolution, chemistry, and life's origins, things got sticky, and there was nothing subtle about Twyla's responses. In retrospect, I should have seen it coming. When I introduced Darwin and evolution, Twyla seemed to bristle. Her visage darkened and she stopped taking notes. On the first test I asked the requisite questions designed to elicit my students' understanding of how evolution works. One of the questions was: "Use the reasoning of natural selection to explain how a flying bass might represent the beginning of a new species." The answer is that the bass would be the progenitor of a new species only if its flying ability gave it some survival advantage over bass that could not fly.

Twyla saw it differently. She wrote: "God made the bass. There is no such thing as a flying bass."

So.

I had no choice but to note on her test, "Your answer does not relate to the question." I did not give her any credit for what she had written. There were a couple of other answers in the same vein—invoking the deity in lieu of scientific reasoning. For these she also received no credit.

Curiously, when I returned her test, Twyla had no response. She simply left the room at the end of the period.

At this point I had a choice: leave it up to her to approach me, or make an honest pedagogical inquiry into the results of the test she had barely passed. Curiosity inspired me to do the latter.

In a quiet moment after one of the ensuing classes I took Twyla aside and asked her if she had read the questions she had not really answered. She said that she had, but went on to explain that she had no patience with trying to, as she phrased it, "translate God's plan into the language of science."

It was an interesting response. Although I thought Twyla was misapprehending the whole intent of science, her comment was articulate. Be this as it may, the question being begged was why she was taking biology if she thought that science contravened the wishes of the Almighty. I put this question to her. She shrugged and told me that her program of study required one science course and mine seemed like the easiest to pass.

I looked at her and said two words: "Brace yourself."

In previous semesters I had had students who were so uninformed about science that it was as if I were asking them to read Sanskrit. Others had talked themselves into the impossibility of their being able to learn science. But I had never had a student who mounted a preemptive strike against it. Until Twyla.

Having such a student in class was stressful, because I knew that Twyla was hearing—and rejecting—almost every word I uttered. How did I know? Because she had ceased taking notes (if, in fact, that was what she had been doing in the first place) and simply sat there, slowly shaking her head, the message being, "Surely, Professor Klose, you of all people must know how terribly mistaken you are."

Inevitably, a second test rolled around. It dealt with ecosystems: plant and animal relationships, who eats who, where energy goes, etc. After the last student had left the room I closed the door and pulled out Twyla's test. To say that my heart sank would be trite. I suppose I was, at some level, prepared for what I saw: many of her answers were phrased in scriptural terms. For example, I asked the students to analyze a given food chain with regard to energy flow: why did populations decrease in size as one ascended a food chain? The answer is that only a fraction of the energy, say, in a population of grass can be passed up the line to a population of rabbits. Therefore, there are fewer rabbits than grass plants in a given environment. Twyla had a different take on this. She wrote, "Everything has its appointed place, designated by the hand of God."

I have, on occasion, run into teachers who say they agonize over students who give irrelevant answers. I was not one of them. Rather than scrawl an apologia about why her answer was not acceptable, I drew a line through it and wrote in a zero. I did the same for several of her other answers, including the one that addressed, or was supposed to address, the question, "Why don't lions, sharks and similar predators have predators of their own?" Twyla: "It is His will."

Need I mention that Twyla and I had another talk? This time I pointed out to her that if she continued on her present course she would fail the class. She sat in my office, gazing at me, as if I had not made a bit of sense. "Why," she asked, "should I write things that I don't approve of?"

"At the risk of alienating you even further," I replied, "approval has nothing to do with it."

For the first time she seemed aghast, sitting bolt upright in her seat, her eyes wide open. "How can you say such a thing?" she protested.

"Twyla," I said, "A biology course is not a test of what you believe to be true. My only concern is that you show understanding of the material. My God, I can understand Hitler's insane rationale for invading Poland without approving of it."

At this point I winced, because I hated analogies that invoked the Nazis. But, like baying hounds, my words had been released, and all I could do was run after them to see where they led me. As it turned out, Twyla didn't seem affronted or offended by what I had said. Instead, she set off in a curious direction: she began to tell me about her life. In an age where the social landscape is littered with catastrophes posing as families, I still felt some compassion for this woman who, to make a long story short, had probably never been loved. She was in her thirties now, and was deeply attached to a small, isolated splinter church in the Maine hinterlands that she had run to when she was twelve to escape the horrors of her home life. This church became her family and the force that had whipped her into white heat about all things intellectual. In the world from which she hailed, curiosity not only killed the cat, but it condemned it to an eternity scratching about in the coal ash of Gehenna. I made no comments about her background, but I did suggest she consider dropping my course, which had become all but a hopeless cause due to her self-destructive approach to it.

"I have to take a science," she said, echoing what she had previously told me about her program requirements.

"Nobody has to do anything," I responded, "aside from obeying the law and not hurting other people." And then I ventured onto her turf by asking, "Twyla, do you think science shouldn't ask these questions?"

To her credit, she gave the question some thought, tipping her head to the side as if waiting for someone to whisper into her ear. She finally said, "Yes."

"Then," I countered, "why does God let us learn these things?"

Twyla shook her head, not so much to disagree with me as to give the impression that she was dispelling wayward thoughts. She got up and left.

Another complication of Twyla's single-minded way of seeing the world was that the other students got wind of her attitude and quietly avoided working with her in the laboratory. So there she sat, alone, making token efforts to set up her lab equipment and nudge some data out of it. But she was easily frustrated. Once, when I was helping her focus her microscope on a cell, I could feel her at the edge of tears when she simply couldn't see what she needed to see. And the more I tried to help her, the more frustrated she became. "Twyla," I said, "just relax. I have all the time you need. You'll get it right. Everybody eventually does. You won't be the first to fail." Finally, after some twenty minutes of fiddling with the controls, she saw a perfect nucleus in one of her own cheek cells, seated like royalty at the center of its little universe of cytoplasm. And then, at that moment, I heard Twyla utter a word that gave me reason for hope. Softly, almost under her breath, she said, "Pretty."

I wanted to say to her that it was okay that the nucleus was pretty, that it was just fine with God that cells had little lives of their own that could be examined through a man-made lens, that they inhaled oxygen and exhaled carbon dioxide and absorbed sugar and created energy and reproduced. These things were okay, and wasn't it wonderful that we had minds that could understand all of this and pass the information on to our children? I wanted to say this, but I didn't. Instead, I walked over to help another student, leaving Twyla to try to complete the work on her own, now that she had taken the first step.

If I were writing a type of hopeful, sentimental fiction, I would go on to say that Twyla's nucleus moment had been her epiphany and that the scales had fallen from her eyes, her true genius had been stimulated, and she had jettisoned her fundamentalism in favor of a rationalist ethic, becoming my prize student and going on to a Ph.D. in biology.

Of course, this didn't happen. It was as if Twyla, salmon-like, had spent all of her energy in the utterance of the word "pretty," after which she died back to her old ways. Nowhere was this more powerfully revealed to me than in her next test, which included a section on chemistry. Such a lovely science, with its little solar system atomic models, its balanced equations, and the alchemy of turning one substance into another. Chemistry, too, was pretty, but Twyla never saw this. When, on the test, I asked why the first atomic shell could hold a maximum of only two electrons, Twyla wrote, "Like the planets, the electrons were put in place by HIS hand, and that's where they shall stay, forever and ever."

It was clear that Twyla's fate in the course was now irrevocable. There were no more probing conversations between us, no further attempts to help her distinguish between demonstrating understanding of an idea and swearing allegiance to it. She rolled into the final exam, expecting . . . well, who knows what? She answered so many questions with biblical quotes and scriptural allusions that I had no choice but to fail her. That meant that she failed the entire course as well, and I didn't anguish over assigning her the grade she had worked so hard to earn.

During the few days of clean-up after the end of the semester I busied myself in my office, tackling backlogged correspondence, clearing my desk, and fielding post-game student questions by e-mail ("Is it too late for me to do extra credit?"). I was surprised when Twyla appeared in the doorway. "How did I do on the final?" she asked.

The question astounded me. How could she have no sense of how she did? "Well," I said, "you failed."

"You mean you failed me," she countered, ever ready for battle.

"All right," I said, "I failed you. I gave you a failing grade."

She firmed her lips. "What about the course?" she asked, reaching out for a life ring.

"You failed," I said.

I expected her to argue with me. But she didn't. Instead, all she asked was, "Why?"

Knowing that anything I said at this point would be mere repetition, I thought for a moment and then told her, "Because the hand of the teacher is a mighty hand, and his judgments righteous."

She said nothing, left the room and, eventually, her program and the school.

Over the ensuing days I found myself wondering what becomes of such students. Where do they go? How do they prosper? How do they come to grips with a world that is increasingly technological? I have never learned the answers to these questions. Maybe because there are things that I, too, do not want to know. ✿

✿ ✿ ✿ ✿ ✿ ✿ ✿ ✿ ✿ ✿ ✿ ✿ ✿ ✿ ✿ ✿ ✿

the dyspepsia of intelligent design

The student was respectful, soft-spoken, and bright. After my first evolution lecture he approached my desk and laid a typewritten paper on it. "You might be interested in this," he said. "It's something my father wrote." Then he left.

I didn't look at that paper until later in the day. And when I did begin to read it I wasn't sure what I was looking at. Full of scientific references to Darwin, natural selection, and genetics, it read like a scientific article but also had the feel of clouds gathering in preparation for rain. And, sure enough, the storm broke on page five with a metaphor about a rhetorical individual's finding a watch, noting its complex workings, and concluding that some intelligent being had constructed it. Ipso facto, thus it is with the natural world: so complex that some higher intelligence must have laid it all out on a celestial drafting table.

The student came to my office several days later and asked me what I thought. "It was an interesting paper," I told him. "Is your father a scientist?"

"No," he said. "He trucks wood."

"He writes well."

The student pressed me. "But what did you think?"

I didn't want to be coy with someone so bright, so I decided to respect his intelligence by stating my appraisal without elaboration. "I can't agree with his analogy. Nature is not a watch. A watch is a man-made device that will always be a watch, no matter how the environment around it changes. But the environment is critical to evolution. It's the engine that drives natural selection."

As was his nature, the student listened attentively and said little. After I had concluded, he nodded and left. He never raised the subject again. The subject, by the way, is the semantic successor to creationism called "intelligent design" (ID)—the idea that living things are the products not of natural forces acting around us but of a superior intelligence. The word "God" is never mentioned.

Of course, proponents of ID are not suggesting that life on earth was initiated and diversified by aliens. There is an unspoken understanding that God, indeed, is the locomotive force, but that by not invoking the deity, ID will have more cachet with the scientific community and will be able to insert itself seamlessly into the science classroom, to coexist on an equal footing with evolution.

I think I prefer the blunt onslaught of good, old-fashioned creationism to the stealth and feinting maneuvers of intelligent design, if only because creationism is bold and straightforward and I know where I stand with it. I'm very uncomfortable with ideas like ID that have aspects that are not enunciated, the same way that Harry Potter is impatient when someone refers to Voldemort as "He who must not be named."

Intelligent design may have gained traction when President George W. Bush was asked if it should be taught in the schools. He responded, ". . . both sides ought to be properly taught." Unwittingly, the president had put his finger squarely on the problem. While intelligent design is indeed a "side" of what is really a social issue, and not at all scientific, evolution is a scientific concept that rests upon mountains of evidence garnered by the sweat of generations of researchers all over the world. In short, the two ideas are not equals, any more than astronomy and astrology are equally legitimate approaches to understanding the workings of the cosmos.

This, then, is intelligent design's first problem: it harbors an ulterior motive. Science is, by necessity, dispassionate, generating data that is thrown into the crucible of the scientific community's critical appraisal. If the data withstands the onslaught of attempts to disprove it, great. If not, then that is also great, because the data was probably weak to begin with. But intelligent design is, by contrast, passionate. It is a plea to see things a certain way or risk the consequences. There are no data to challenge. Either one believes or—gulp—doesn't.

But there is a more elementary problem with intelligent design, a semantic problem that should be the starting point of its deconstruction. This is the redundancy of the term itself, to wit: how can design be anything but intelligent? The very word "design" indicates an intent to lay things out in some manner that is logical, consistent, and whole. After all, there is no such thing as "unintelligent design." At the risk of aiding and abetting the efforts of ID promoters, "Creation by design" would be a better attempt to inflict psychic and pedagogical pain upon the Godless evolutionists. But then the sticky word "Creation" would have to be grappled with, and we are back where we started.

Beyond terminology, intelligent design presents another difficulty—the "moving target" issue. When science bumps up against something it doesn't understand, it experiments until answers erupt. Intelligent design, by contrast, attributes confounding phenomena to the mystery of unknowable intent by a superior intelligence. But when science finally is able to explain the subject that had stymied it, intelligent design must "shift down the line" to the next unknown. For example, there was a time when scientists did not understand how the immune system recognized cancer cells, or whether it recognized them at all. The path of least resistance was to say that it was a mystery, part of the universal design of things; or worse, that cancer was a punishment inflicted by a vengeful deity for sinful transgressions. But now that we do have an idea how cancer cells look to our immune cells, intelligent design must shift its focus to the next unknown, because it contains no mechanism for arriving at answers.

This is exactly the way it was with heredity. In the seventeenth century, the Dutch mathematician Nicolas Hartsoeker observed human semen with a microscope and postulated that there must be a very tiny human being curled up in the head of each sperm cell. He called these "homunculi" (literally "little men," though one assumes they could just as easily have been little women).

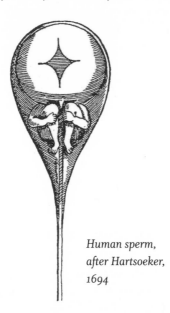

Human sperm,
after Hartsoeker,
1694

This observation jibed nicely with the prevailing belief of the time that the woman's uterus was a passive receptacle and incubator for the essence of the future child delivered to her by the male. This idea was so sacrosanct that attempts by inquiring minds to explain heredity in coldly mechanical terms were furiously quashed by the Church. This brings us to perhaps the greatest irony in all of science history — that the laws of sex were eventually figured out by a monk.

Gregor Mendel was an Augustinian friar who lived in a monastery in what is now the Czech Republic. Born to a peasant family laboring under the feudal system, he was a poor book learner who spoke coarse German and only passable Czech. Although he never met Darwin, he had read *The Origin of Species* and noted this telling passage: "The laws of heredity are for the most part unknown." In other words, while Darwin brilliantly explained why certain traits are passed from generation to generation, he couldn't explain how this might occur. This was because Darwin had math anxiety and was ill equipped to take the quantitative approach necessary to tackle the problem of heredity. This was left to Mendel, who immediately recognized the need for masses of data, derived from thousands of cross-breeding experiments, to generate the statistical evidence needed to prove that reproduction was not a 100/0 affair but rather an equitable 50/50, with both male and female making equal genetic contributions to the offspring. He chose pea plants for his subjects, which allowed him to perform multitudes of crosses simultaneously and in a relatively small amount of space. When Mendel finally published his results, most scientists didn't understand his mathematical explanation of heredity, and the scientific world went on for another thirty years believing that the uterus was merely an incubator. But when it did finally recognize the epoch-making importance of Mendel's work, it in effect acknowledged that heredity had been liberated from the prison of mysticism. Those who only grudgingly accepted Mendel's conclusions now had to look elsewhere to affix the label of "mystery" or "unknowable" to other, as yet unsolved, problems surrounding heredity.

Intelligent design's greatest shortcoming, then, is that it is intellectually trivial. It asks nothing of us in the way of critical thought. But I am especially disappointed when my students purvey it. On one occasion, as with the student who gave me his father's paper, one of them suggested that ID is suitable ersatz for evolution because it (1) sounds scientific and (2) does not (wink) mention God. Yet they know, and I know, and everybody knows, that (3) it was concocted as a way to get religion into the science classroom, and (4) that one of the commandments is "Thou shalt not lie." In any case, it is being sold as scientific for those who want to "feel" that they are doing science but are averse to the heavy lifting of experimentation.

What's disarming about intelligent design is the relatively low-level nature of the sell. I have been screamed at by creationists, but intelligent designers are more reasonable. They don't damn me, but rather convey an almost parental sense of disappointment in my wayward belief in evolution, expressing the hope that I will one day see the light. When, in rebuttal, I state the case for Darwin, they become dyspeptic, as if I intended to upset them, but they never lose control. They simply soldier on. Their message of intelligent design is delivered by snail mail, e-mail, through the occasional student, and in a door-to-door fashion, as happened one day when two impeccably dressed men came to my office to ask that I include intelligent design in my biology course. They even handed me the text I could use. I respectfully paged through it, then handed it back. "There is no science here," I said. And then I went on to suggest that there was probably a place for intelligent design in a course on current events, or in a philosophy or theology course, although the theologians might become impatient with the superficial secularity of ID and the acrobatics it goes through to avoid mentioning God. One of the men then accused me of intolerance.

Am I intolerant? Only if I am shirking some presumed duty to entertain every suggestion for the origin and diversity of life on earth, no matter how unscientific. But that's not my job. Above all else, my responsibility is to remain relevant to the subject matter. When I was a student, I occasionally had teachers who, as they used to say, "went off on tangents." By no stretch of the imagination did their vignettes and laments about faculty–administrator politics or the woeful ignorance of us students relate to the theme of the course. More often than not, these were poor, self-indulgent teachers, but being a dutiful student, I sat and listened until I got my B. The most important lesson I learned from them, now that I am a teacher myself, is that I must take care to keep my eye on the topical compass. I allow the needle to waver at times, but I always return to true north. To wedge intelligent design into my class would be like reversing the magnetic poles: I would no longer know where I was, and I would be taking the class with me. And then there's the issue of unfairness to my students. If I were to throw intelligent design into the works, I would be communicating an inconsistency: that most scientific phenomena are explicable in terms of conclusions based on data, but the origin and diversification of life forms is a matter of faith.

I attended a Catholic high school in New Jersey. My biology teacher was a monk with a Socratic gift for teaching. His was the directive influence in my decision to become a biologist. I knew nothing about evolution or natural selection before taking his class. He opened my eyes to a kaleidoscopic world of countless and intricate life forms and remarkable order. He could demonstrate mitosis — cell division — with his fingers and, in the days before PowerPoint, outline the complexities of protein synthesis on the blackboard. I came away from his class with biology in my bones, driven to explore and experiment. It struck me only in retrospect that Brother Richard never paused in the middle of his talk on Darwin to remark, "Of course, we all know who's really responsible for all these different species." Rather, he stuck to his science, and in so doing, escorted us milk-faced sophomores to a point of departure to assess our own understanding and draw our own conclusions. This is all that education is supposed to do. Everything else is extraneous.

Intelligent design can do nothing to improve upon this approach. It adds nothing to scientific understanding, just as the irrelevant anecdotes of some of my undergraduate professors did nothing to highlight the course material. I explained this, quietly and diplomatically, to the two gentlemen sitting, with high hopes, in my office. My reluctance to cooperate frustrated them. But when they left they magnanimously handed the intelligent design text back to me as a gift, "in the faith," as one put it, "that it will eventually open your eyes."

To this day, it has still not had the desired effect. ♣

※ ※ ※ ※ ※ ※ ※ ※ ※ ※ ※ ※ ※ ※ ※ ※ ※

the skeptic

When I was an undergraduate student in marine biology, doing a semester of coursework in the Virgin Islands (how one martyrs oneself for science), everyone in my class, as a sort of capstone project, had to plan, carry out, write up, and publicly present an original experiment — in the space of four weeks. We were a talented and enthusiastic lot of early twenty-somethings, so we went about the work with élan.

My partner and I, for example, examined the symbiotic relationship between a small, defenseless, and probably blind crab and a large sea urchin, *Meoma ventricosa*. Another team examined the nocturnal migratory behavior of barracuda; while another concocted a set-up to raise seaweeds in processed sewage water.

But the experiment that caught my eye was one that was constructed by a couple of fun-loving women in the class. In between marathon games of poolside bridge, they occasionally arose — as languidly as mist on a lake — to examine their project. This consisted of a large, wooden, Y-shaped trough of seawater (a so-called "Y-maze"). Their subject was a solitary sea urchin (*Diadema antillarum*) with exceptionally long, barbed spines. (Upon our arrival in St. Croix, the professors had cautioned us against so much as touching this urchin, for the brittle, barbed spines embedded themselves deeply and painfully. Shortly after this cautionary lecture, I slipped in the water and sat on one.)

In each of the arms of the "Y" the women placed a different species of alga. Then they placed the unwitting urchin at the far end of the stem of the Y. Over the course of hours, and if it were so inclined, the urchin made its way, laboriously, up the Y, to the fork, where it would—one hoped—choose one alga over the other to graze upon. It was the perfect endeavor for budding scientists-cum-bridge-players, for it required only that one look at the experiment every few hours, then check off the appropriate alga as selected by the urchin.

The thing was, every so often the urchin got to the fork in the Y and halted. At this point a crowd of students would gather, in sympathetic psychic vibration with the two women, willing the urchin to make a move one way or the other. (On one occasion one of the students, unable to bear up under the frustration of the invertebrate's indecisiveness, shouted, "Choose!" He startled everyone but the urchin.)

But there was another way.

If the urchin kept the women away from their bridge game for too long, one of them would gently rock the trough of seawater. More often than not, this would be enough to stir the urchin from its lethargy, making it list toward a particular alga (usually the one toward which the rocking of the trough had nudged it). Then they would note the result, resettle the urchin at the far end of the trough (but gently!) and return to their card table (*avec* piña coladas).

There is a moral here, and it is this: in science there are terrible pressures to produce results. These pressures, for the most part, are known as tenure, grant money, publication, and competition with colleagues. What this means is that, in the course of an experiment, a researcher, sensing that he or she "knows" what the outcome will be, occasionally hurries things along by "jostling the urchin."

(There are stellar historical examples of this. Gregor Mendel, the monk who discovered how sex worked, is thought to have been somewhat "loose" at times in the interpretation of his observations in order to make his numbers jibe. Pasteur and Newton have also been targets of similar allegations.)

I'm not talking about outright fraud here, but rather something far more visceral and human; that is, seduction: yielding to the siren call of success, which brings with it—in one fell swoop—collegial esteem, an improved curriculum vitae, and the all-important funding, among other dollops of approbation.

A case in point is one I cite again and again in my biology courses: The Mars Rock.

Back in 1996, a four-and-a-half-pound rock was found in Antarctica. It was judged to have emanated from Mars and fallen to earth some thirteen thousand years ago (Mark Twain might have added, "come September 5th"). Electron microscopy revealed what looked like petrified bacteria deep inside the stone. Scientists announced, with minimal restraint, that these tiny structures represented life forms (bacteria?) that had flourished at a time when Mars was a kinder and gentler place. The news services reported the announcement with unbridled enthusiasm and before long there were mobs nodding sagely that life, in fact, had been found on Mars.

Let me set the record straight. As of this writing, life is not known to exist on Mars. Further, there is no evidence that it ever existed. Disappointing, but true. Will we some day find life, fossil or living, on Mars? I don't know.

With these three words—I—don't—know—I have spoken in the best tradition of science: I have reserved judgment pending compelling evidence.

The business of science is skepticism. So what happened with the Mars rock? I saw the photographs of the meteorite's innards and I, too, could have interpreted the tiny, crusty tubules as microbes, if that's what I wanted them to be. But at the time I felt less strong about the possibility of their representing ancient life forms than I did about the probability that they were not. (In fact, the Mars rock fever soon broke, and an immense question mark now hovers over the thing, as it should.)

Science has waxed poetic about first impressions before, and on more than one occasion. Take "polywater," for example. In 1968 the first reports appeared in reputable scientific journals that an alternative form of water had been discovered, more viscous than the regular stuff that runs out of our taps. For four years the fear grew that if polywater were to escape from the laboratory it could proselytize normal water, ending life on earth as we know it. In the end, it turned out that polywater was simply water with impurities.

"Mitogenic rays" were another orthodoxy foisted upon uncritical observers by legitimate scientists. The idea here was that plants — such as onions — gave off growth-stimulating rays that affected the onions around them, "unless a plate of glass were placed between them." Although the existence of these mysterious rays was eventually disproved, papers continued to be published for many years.

Anyone out and about in the early 1990s may remember the "cold fusion" fiasco. First, a little background. Nuclear power plants produce energy by splitting atoms. This process is known as "fission." It creates monstrous amounts of power, but also a lot of radioactive waste. Fusion, by contrast, involves the *smooshing together* of atoms. This also produces a lot of energy, but the bonus — and the importance of this bonus cannot be overemphasized — is that it is waste-free, so the government doesn't have to bribe a state to bury it for thousands of years until it stops glowing. (Point of interest: the sun is a huge fusion reactor, in which hydrogen atoms are fused together to make slightly larger helium atoms. Some day the sun will run out of hydrogen and the reactor will shut down. As this happens, the sun will become a "red giant," bloating until it embraces the earth, turning us into a cinder.)

Now, there are no workable fusion reactors on earth because

they require very high temperatures. But in the early 1990s two men—their names shall live in infamy—claimed to have constructed a mini-fusion reactor on a tabletop, at room temperature. This so-called "cold fusion" device required the use of the metal palladium. Once again, the news services drank it up (and palladium futures skyrocketed). A Nobel Prize seemed assured. Our energy woes vanquished! The trouble was, other scientists were unable to reproduce these results, and the cold fusion idea died a quick death. (Now the plan for meeting our energy needs has miserably turned to clean-burning coal.)

How does all this relate to college science teaching? Well, directly. Imparting information and encouraging science literacy is only half of my job. The other half is encouraging skepticism. Especially about new ideas. This is the whole purpose of the scientific method: test—observe—repeat, over and over. The great ideas of science are truly the cream of this regimen. The Cell Theory, the Uncertainty Principle, Relativity, Natural Selection. All have held up really well under the relentless assault of inquiring minds and probing instrumentation. If a great idea, or any idea, passes scrutiny again and again, well, good for the idea. And if it fails? Well, good for scrutiny—the idea deserved to die; in which case, good for science, good for us. What's the point in having sloppy, crapped-up thinking that hasn't gone through the crucible mixed in with concepts that have suffered slings and arrows, fire and sword, and come out of the fray standing on their own two feet? It's this poor understanding of what science is that brings "Creation science" hokum into the classroom masquerading as the product of hard-nosed experimental inquiry.

My approach to my students has taken the form of a periodic charge, in which I stand before them and point an accusing finger. "Challenge me," I tell them. "Use your noggins, and the information you now have, and tell me how these ideas might not be true. Make me earn my pay." (Once, in my marine biology course, I was lecturing on how lunar gravity influences the tides. A student raised her hand. "I find it hard to believe in gravity," she said, "because there doesn't seem to be any way to measure it." Wonderful! In fact, gravity may be a concept on the verge of extinction, in favor of Einstein's idea about warps in the space–time continuum.)

In this light, one of the most unnerving things for this science teacher is the sight of my students scribbling away as I lecture, living not by Coke and Doritos alone but by every word that comes out of my mouth. Of course, some concepts, such as "cells," don't leave much room for debate; but ideas like the inheritance of personality traits, biochemical signaling in cancer cells, and evolution, have very soft margins, leaving ample space for exploration and, if one is lucky, the generation of new observations and ideas. One never knows what one will come up with unless one makes a conscious decision to think rather than simply recite what one has heard.

Sometimes, carefully, I remark to my students that, of all Jesus' apostles, I find Thomas the most interesting. When Christ reappeared after his crucifixion, the other apostles, though fearful at first, quickly came to joy. But Thomas was the holdout. He wanted to put his fingers in Christ's wounds. Then he would believe. Thomas, in short, was the scientist of the group.

Which brings me back to the Mars rock. When news of it broke, the general approbation left me shaking my head. Science is not supposed to be a tent revival where the password for inclusion is "Amen." I was willing, after thoughtful consideration, to admit that there was, without doubt, something interesting in the rock. That this something was once living is worthy of doubt. Doubting is much more scientific than the hallelujahs that initially echoed through the press and for which the Mars rock scientists should feel, to some extent, abashed.

If and when these Martian "bacteria" are validated, I will walk the receiving line and shake deserving hands. But, having congratulated the victors, I will also keep an unscientific speculation to myself. I have sometimes thought that, eons ago, before there was any life here, an alien race of giants seeded our world, making earth its garden in the galactic countryside. Some day, these giants are going to return. When they do, they're going to look at the place and exclaim, "Damn! We've got humans." Then they'll spray.

And that will be the end of us. ♣

the three-legged woman and the imp of the paranormal

In my course in introductory biology I include a few lectures on the structure of the atom as a basis for understanding the chemistry of living things. In an effort to convey how incredibly small these particles are, I point out that although the modern atomic model was described by the brilliant Danish physicist Niels Bohr in 1913, we were not able to actually see an atom until the 1980s, when researchers at IBM photographed atoms using a new invention called the Scanning Tunneling Microscope. Soon after—as a sort of encore—this instrument was used to *manipulate* thirty-five atoms of the gas xenon—and later, the very heavy metal thorium—into a pattern, a corporate logo to be exact. And which logo would that be?

Why, IBM, of course.

When I tell my students about this, many—but not all—of them are duly wowed. On one occasion, a young man spoke up and decreed that atoms did not exist. His reasoning: if they were so elusive and virtually invisible, how could they constitute substances as dense as metals? Further, he asked how such exceedingly small things—mere will 'o the quantum wisps—could be shuffled around, even by IBM?

I would like to begin by reaffirming my belief that skepticism is necessary in any discipline, but especially in science, where experimental findings must rest upon a veritable Masada of data if they are to be taken seriously by the scientific community. It is the duty of every scientist worth his or her salt to listen to new information with an attentive but always critical ear. For every nod of the head as one considers a new piece of data, there should be four or five impatient taps of the pencil upon the desktop (I think this is the correct ratio). The result is a set of results that emerges from the crucible of cross-examination, ready for general dissemination.

In short, I, like most teachers I know, encourage critical thinking in my classes.

"Dissect the knowledge, don't worship it," I tell my students. Challenge me. Ask questions. Hold me to account for what I teach. (Niels Bohr used to tell his students, "Every sentence that I utter should be regarded by you not as an assertion but as a question.") This is, more or less, what my student, that atom-doubter, did, and although it would have been nice if he hadn't ruled out the existence of atoms with such finality, how could I object to his putting my intellectual feet to the fire and compelling me to explain the concept further, to the point where understanding was a real possibility?

However, I was troubled by his tendency—shared by other of my students over the years—to reject scientific information out of hand. Atoms, genetics, plate tectonics, evolution (especially evolution!)—all have fallen victim not only to their doubts, but to outright disbelief. They are not usually hostile to the information; they simply convey the impression that I must be, somehow, mistaken.

This I can live with. What bamboozles me—and this is the main point at which I have long last arrived—is that the same students who sniff at the role DNA plays in determining our physical and, to an extent, behavioral characteristics frequently embrace paranormal and even atrocious, *Enquirer*-caliber claims whole hog. Secret human/animal hybrid experiments, crop circles, Martian civilizations, invisible atmospheric jellyfish creatures, and jackalopes make their way down my students' mental gullets without a hitch. Why, I once asked myself, if they are willing to accept such unsubstantiated things at face value, can't they at least be receptive to that which has been arrived at via the scientific method? How can a student doubt that the continents are adrift, yet seize the idea of alien abductions with such dire passion?

This very thought was brought home to me in spades some years ago when I was walking the minefield of evolution in my general biology course. I recall a student, Ian, who, when I described the evolution of the modern horse from a small, puppy dog-size ancestor, expressed his skepticism (using the words "You've got to be kidding" for emphasis); but when I asked if anyone could describe the evolution of another species, it was Ian himself who raised his hand and uttered the following, which I shall never forget: "I once saw a three-legged woman in a porno magazine. It was amazing. I said to myself, is this evolution?"

At first I thought he was joking, so I smiled benignly and stared into the distance. But his comment had electrified the class (late on a Friday afternoon, when they were normally as torpid as clams at low tide). They became intensely interested in this unfortunate woman, and fell into animated chatter, wanting to know where they could get hold of the magazine that contained the corroborating image.

I eventually brought the class under control, although some grew resentful when I discounted Ian's story. The thing was, he had been absolutely serious (I can still see his face, earnest and open, seeking only my approval). In fact, if our classroom had been a ship, the crew of students, given a choice between my navigational course and the one Ian had set, would have strung me up from the yardarm and awarded him sash and sword.

Evolution is not the only thing that brings out false as well as fabulous associations in students' minds. It is the same with many other areas of science, especially if they are theoretical or cutting-edge: real-world scientific goings-on incur student doubt, while their faith in the fringe and paranormal aspects of science remains boundless. Thus, when I address the conditions that promote human twinning, my students assail me with questions about Siamese twins conjoined at the genitalia; when I describe the mechanics of cloning simple cells, they profess that the government has been secretly cloning human automatons for years, ready to do society's drudge work while the rest of us lead lives of indolence; when I outline the mechanisms of genetic mutation, the word "mutation" conjures in my students visions of someone sprouting a second head (in the grotesque manner of the classic 1950s sci-fi flick, *The Manster*).

In Ian's very same class, when I announced that we would be studying chemistry for the next two weeks, as preamble to the biological topics to follow, a hand immediately flagged me. The question: "Are we going to blow things up?"

There it is, then. Science seldom involves "blowing things up." Although many scientific ideas are explosive in their implications, the research work leading up to a data-based conclusion involves a tremendous amount of tedium (that is, somebody has got to wash those damn test tubes and crunch those numbers). What's more, in order to achieve a reasonable grasp of a scientific concept, some depth of understanding — education — is in order. Thus, the *idea* of the sheer diversity of life on earth is startling, but a discussion of the mechanisms and conditions that made that life possible in the first place involves an understanding of atomic bonding, thermodynamics, and gas exchange across the cell membrane. Most of these processes cannot be *seen* in any direct way: oxygen and carbon dioxide are invisible; microscopes (even IBM's) are not yet powerful enough to resolve atomic *structure*; and heat can only be felt (and imaged in the abstract). However, these things are measurable, but measurement involves numbers and instrumentation and time and . . . well, you get the picture. Science is *hard*.

In contrast to mainstream science, paranormal phenomena do have the effect of "blowing things up," because they offer big, grand, gorgeous images that even the uninitiated can grasp and thrill to at first blush. It makes little difference if one has never seen Bigfoot, an alien, or a human clone. There are those who claim they have, and many, many others are anxious to vouch for their existence by proxy.

The paranormal, in short, promises absolute answers in the here and now. It belongs to popular, not scientific, culture. As such, it offers all that the grind of scientific research does not: immediate gratification, pat explanations, and the reduction of complex matters to fleeting sound and image bites. This expectation of ready answers is poor preparation for a scientific vocation, where the measured steps of laboratory research are often less than thrilling and their denouement seldom gripping. But to precipitate an extraterrestrial as a substitute for an understanding of the physics underlying astronomy—now, that's science as popular culture likes it: low calorie, low carb, yet sweet.

The problem is that popular culture, while seductive and fleetingly satisfying, is not transmissible. Check that. What I mean is that there is no value in transmitting it. Consider: what father would sit his five-year-old son upon his knee and begin, "Now, Ernest, let's talk about UFOs so that, some day, you can tell your children what we know about the universe." But the transmission of real science improves us as a species. Lacking instinct as we do, it's the only option for the constructive development of modern society, which has become, for better and sometimes worse, a technocracy.

The upshot of all this is that the far greater allure of the paranormal and pseudoscientific has impeded students' ability to grapple with the concepts and precepts of so-called "hard science." This brings them only frustration and desperation when they are confronted with ideas that (1) demand that they think, (2) are perceived as irrelevant to their experience, and (3) like Darwin's theory of natural selection, depend to some extent on inference and deductive reasoning. Thus, they are unwilling to believe that humans descended from a lower order of animals, yet they are already sold on our species' evolutionary future, where they envision throbbing buttheads suspended in the universal ether, radiating lethal levels of IQ, and communicating with one another via telepathy. It's much less stressful to embrace such a fantastic idea, because it is intellectually lax, requires no dreaded math, and offers the *sense* that one is dabbling in the scientific. Aficionados of this stuff can find no comfortable place to sit at the banquet of mainstream science, so they sate themselves with McScience, emphasizing convenience and speed over diet.

This imp of the paranormal bites students with the tenacity of a deer tick and persists like Lyme disease; but the students are weakened by it because it convinces them that knowledge is easy to come by. The teacher interested in turning back this tide of ignorance might, as a first plan of assault, quote Einstein, who said, "As the diameter of a circle of light increases, so does the circumference of darkness around it." What he was alluding to, of course, was that the more we learn, the more questions we raise. (Mark Twain struck the same theme in a more jocose way when he wrote, "Scientists have raised so many questions about the subject that we shall soon know nothing about it at all.") The challenge is to convey this to students without frustrating them, to portray science as an invitation rather than the labor of Sisyphus. The dedicated and creative teacher knows what to do.

Which leaves me with several questions: If UFOs have visited earth, why do they always abduct a bumpkin sitting in a rowboat in the middle of Maine? Why don't they ever take a surgeon? Or a president? Why don't they ever take *me*? ❧

boundless moments

✻ ✻ ✻ ✻ ✻ ✻ ✻ ✻ ✻ ✻ ✻ ✻ ✻ ✻ ✻ ✻ ✻
let us praise the bold molds

It's that time of the semester again, the point in my college biology course when I must scramble, in the dead of winter, to grow fungi for my students.

To most, it's not a very appealing notion; but to a biologist the fungi are as beautiful as they are intriguing.

Delicate as cotton wisps, or tough as leather, each species of fungus has its own very narrow preferences for growing conditions — temperature, humidity, light, and substrate — which allow it to blossom forth, often explosively. Who hasn't discovered, on a damp autumn morning, the lawn, or that shade under a pine tree, studded with mushrooms that weren't there the day before? I recall, many years back, reading about some Long Island homeowners who awoke one day to find translucent, coconut-size globes on their front lawns. What's more, these spheres seemed to drift across the grass of their own accord. The claim took fire that these entities were from outer space, an assertion that the media seized upon, to the confusion of everybody. This only pointed up, for me, how easy it is to incite fear when one's raw material is ignorance.

The Long Island fungus phenomenon highlighted the one enduring truth common to all fungi: when conditions are just right, they will not be daunted. There's a story about a New Jersey man who discovered that mushrooms had broken through the hardened asphalt in his driveway. The fellow dug at them, poured lime over them, and even set them on fire, but still they grew. They had to. It was their time. In a contest between man and fungus, the outcome is seldom in doubt.

When I first read this story I wondered how organisms so soft and often mushy could possibly disrupt such a tough man-made material. And then, as if being punished for being an unbeliever, I had my own such experience.

In our backyard we have an asphalt basketball court, laid down in 1994. It served us well for seven years, until, one day in the fall of 2001, I noticed a bulge about eight inches across. Attributing this to the vagaries of Maine weather, I took a sledgehammer and beat the bulge flat. The next morning there were four such bulges. I beat them flat too. The next day, in a scene reminiscent of a Three Stooges plot, there were six. Curious now, I laid my sledgehammer aside and went about my business, wondering what course the bulges might take if left alone. That evening, when I returned, the aliens had broken through into my world. Mushrooms. Big honking things. Plump and white. It was with a heavy heart that I dug them out, filled the holes with herbicide, and patched up the mess. But every now and then, a new bulge appears, letting me know that they're still there. Probing.

Molds, mildews, mushrooms. Fungi all. What they have in common is that they are composed of tiny fibers—hyphae—which in some cases are packed tightly together, as in the mushroom, and in others are as diffuse as pulled cotton, as in some species of bread mold. A determined and patient mycologist (one who studies fungi) once measured the growing tips of all the hyphae of a bread mold and found that, in a single night, they had grown an astounding one *kilometer*.

I often sing the praises of the fungi to my students. Once they get over the unappealing sound of the word, most of them warm to these organisms. Neither plant nor animal, they emulate both: they often look like plants, but, like animals, they must get their food elsewhere, usually from dead or decaying organic matter. Ever wonder why the forest isn't littered with the fallen trunks of dead trees? 'Tis fungi that germinate and spread as soon as (and sometimes before) the sap of these trees has ceased to flow. In fact, even while these trees were young and thriving, their bows aloft, their leaves angled toward the sun, they were literally blanketed with the microscopic spores of fungi. These spores were biding their time, waiting for an opportunity to return the wood's nutrients to the earth from whence they came.

The world of fungi is so vast and complex that I have never found any figure for the number of known species. Part of the problem is that some fungi exist for only a couple of days—long enough to produce their fruiting bodies—and then disappear without a trace. But we do know that, despite their being some of the most primitive organisms on the planet, they have one monumental claim to fame: the largest organism in the world is a fungus. According to the *Canadian Journal of Forest Research*, this behemoth—estimated to be over eight thousand years old—carpets nearly ten square kilometers of Oregon forest floor, an area equivalent to about sixteen hundred football fields.

Still, such impressive facts do not bring fungi close enough to home for my students, so I give it to them in starker and more personal terms: athlete's foot; ringworm; yeast infections; jock itch. These are all parasites, and I hurry to reassure the class that most other fungi are so-called "saprophytes," which while away their days living off dead stuff, presenting no danger to us.

In these days preceding our chapter on the fungi, I find myself busily preparing specimens for my students' study and, I hope, delight. Fungi are big and small, lackluster beige and brilliant-orange, threadlike and buttonlike. And, most importantly, they will "attack" anything of an organic nature. In fact, there is evidence they will grow on just about anything that contains carbon, whether it was once living or not. A friend of mine who had moved to Galveston from the Midwest once left her Texas home for a week and made the mistake of turning off the air conditioning. Upon her return, she discovered that fungi, taking advantage of the sudden heat and humidity, had eaten away the rubber seal on the door of her refrigerator, then had begun to consume the food that lay within. Talk about opportunists.

On those occasions when detractors sniff at my affinity for the fungi, I remind myself—and them—that I am in good company. The poet Frederick George Scott once wrote (albeit in a state of despondency), "Day by day the mould I smell / of this fungus-blistered cell." And the Nobel laureate Seamus Heaney, in his "Personal Helicon," spoke fondly of them:

> As a child, they could not keep me from wells
> And old pumps with buckets and windlasses.
> I loved the dark drop, the trapped sky, the smells
> Of waterweed, fungus and dank moss.

And for those whose reading is restricted to whatever glimmers on the computer screen, there is a wonderful site called "The Norwegian Fungus of the Month."

I don't know why the fungi captivate me the way they do. Perhaps, like those Long Island homeowners, I perceive them as otherworldly. When I want to verify this, I sneak down, flashlight in hand, into the crawlspace under my house. It's a damp, dark, musty chamber with a hardpan floor that turns to mud in the spring (a liability of living on the banks of a river). I always tread carefully, because there are thin, white, veinlike tendrils creeping about in the wet earth. Looking something like the alien appendages in the original film version of *The War of the Worlds*, they are exceedingly delicate. I once accidentally brushed up against such a filament and it collapsed into itself. The next day it was completely gone. I don't know what species this organism is, and I am convinced (based upon my experience of living with it for so long) that it poses no threat to me. My only desire is to periodically acknowledge it, and allow it to go its way.

I have told my students this story, and their response is always a mixture of fascination and a certain curiosity about how I utilize my free time. But I come by my interests honestly. I told them about an incident from my boyhood, my first-ever interaction with a fungus, and it was a lulu.

Growing up in Jersey City in the 1960s, I had a friend down the street, Bobby Slavinski. His parents were accumulators and had pack-ratted their garage full of newspapers, until they stood in tight, dense towers. It was a wonderful, stinking, rotting maze for kids looking for a place to play hide and seek. One day three of us twelve-year-olds ventured into the half-darkness, wrinkled our noses at the smell, and then stopped in our tracks when we saw something resting upon an old *Jersey Journal* bearing news of the election of JFK. It was orange, about the size of a grapefruit, and had folds and sulci, just like a human brain. Inspired, we immediately declared it to be an alien brain. Then I, the intrepid one who wanted to be a scientist one day, took a stick and poked it. Immediately, a cloud of "gas" spewed out. We ran for the street, screaming. (Later on we returned with a BB gun and shot it. There.)

What I know now that I didn't know then was that this "thing" was a fungus. It had blossomed on the damp *Jersey Journal*, taking advantage of just the right combination of temperature, moisture, light, and printer's ink. The "gas" it emitted was its reproductive spores. We eventually returned a third time and shoveled the entity into a pickle jar so that we could take it to Jersey City

State College for identification. But as soon as we emerged into the light of day, it literally fell apart, collapsing into a gooey mess. Hmm. Maybe it *was* an alien brain.

Now I know why, exactly why, the fungi electrify me and make me want to share my enthusiasm with my students. It's because I was fortunate enough to have noticed them all my life, to have interacted with them, to have been affected by them. In all these ways I came to understand them, as far as it is possible for a non-mycologist to do so. Even now, as I write this, it is early July in Maine, and in the woodchips that form the mulch around my privet hedge, there has ascended a handful of gorgeous mushrooms — *Stropharia rugosoannulata* — denoted "delicious" by the *Simon and Schuster's Guide to Mushrooms*. But I do not pick them, despite the temptation. Instead, I lie prone and admire them. Of all places, they have chosen this obscure spot under my privet. I feel more privileged than hungry.

Someday I'd like to teach a course in mycology. But my school is small, and a sufficient number of interested students would not exist to justify it. And so I get in my lessons on the fungi by stealth, as part of the smorgasbord that constitutes a course in general biology. It seems to work just fine this way, and I don't run the risk of alienating students by giving them too much of a good thing. And who knows how many pilot lights of curiosity about the fungi I have lit over the years? One student, many semesters after he had taken my course, appeared in my office one day and, quivering with excitement, took off his shoe and sock. "Look, Professor Klose!" he exclaimed, "*Tinea pedis!*" Oddly, I was flattered.

In the quiet and solitude of an early winter evening after a day of teaching, I take a piece of bread, some orange rind, a dab of marmalade, and a piece of leather from an old shoe. Each of these I place in its individual petri dish. A mist of water from an atomizer before setting the covers down. Then I put these dishes in the darkness of a paper bag and set them on top of the refrigerator, a place of subtle warmth. After a week I open the bag and — *voilà!* — the desert has blossomed like a rose, or rather, like a mold, four separate species to be exact, in colors ranging from black to orange to blue-green.

I have my fungi, and I couldn't be happier. ♣

a season for seaweeds

In poetry, art, and song, the sea is celebrated as having unsurpassed beauty ("I must go down to the sea again, to the lonely sea and the sky" — Masefield); but, truth to tell, there is much in the ocean that is, at first blush, downright ugly — to the uninitiated.

I don't know where the term sea*weed* originated, but it is clear that the person who came up with it harbored little esthetic appreciation for these plants. I, for one, can't seem to get enough of them; and I take pride in having introduced many students to their wiles.

One of the high points of the semester is when I indulge one of my great pleasures — collecting seaweeds for my marine biology class. It is, of course, possible to simply present my students with "pressings" or — gasp — photographs, but what fun would that be? In order to develop esteem for the understated beauty of seaweeds, one must engage them in the slimy flesh, hands on, with eyes, nostrils — and even taste buds — open.

I understand why seaweeds seem to fall comfortably into the category of the "esthetically challenged." The reasons are many. They don't flower, they're slimy, they rot on beaches, and their spectrum of colors is limited to just red, brown, and green, usually in subdued hues. Even some of their names sound disagreeable: *Chondrus*, *Ulva*, *Fucus* (pronounced like "mucus").

This points up one of the problems of getting people to come around to seaweeds. Many seaweeds don't have English, or common, names. But those that do, often have fanciful monikers: there's Irish moss (very tasty), sea colander, knotted wrack, and my favorite—gorilla ogo, an invasive Pacific seaweed that, like the proverbial 600-pound ape, goes wherever it wants.

My students' experiences with seaweeds do nothing to ennoble them. They relate childhood episodes of splatting their siblings with gobs of the stuff. Others describe having smelled it decaying. Now and then I encounter the intrepid soul who has eaten it, vowing never to do so again. Of course, some seaweeds, like kelp, are relished for some quality only an eater of seaweeds could explain.

To me, my students' attitudes toward seaweeds represent nothing less than a challenge. To take something that at first glance seems uninteresting at best, and then reveal the beauty within is, for me, a deeply satisfying aspect of teaching.

As I drive through the low, snow-covered hills along the Penobscot here in central Maine, my anticipation steadily heightens as the river widens toward the bay. I don't know what excites me more, the seaweed or the idea of being absolutely alone on a Maine beach in the very heart of winter. Perhaps it is some intangible combination of the two.

I arrive at Blue Hill Falls at low tide—heaven for the marine biologist in search of algae (did I mention that seaweeds are algae? In short, this simply means no flowers, no roots, no leaves, no internal conducting vessels for water and minerals—just like the stuff that one scrapes off the glass of a home aquarium).

I get out of my truck, put on my rubber calf boots, and crunch through a thin layer of ice as I make my way over the rocks and down to the beach. The cold air smells of salt and I also get a whiff of putrefaction. The seaweeds are near.

My students seldom ask why seaweeds are slimy; they just take it for granted that they are, and that this is part and parcel of their essence. But like everything else in nature, there is rhyme in the slime. It allows the nearshore seaweeds to withstand exposure to air until the tide rises again. Other seaweeds are always submerged and are, consequently, in less need of a protective coating.

I have chosen this collecting day carefully, being sure to arrive at a spring low tide. A spring tide has nothing to do with seasonal spring; rather, it is simply an extreme tide (the water seems to "spring" away from the beach) occurring twice per month. (There is, similarly, a spring high tide, which is a higher-than-normal high tide. This holds little interest for a man in pursuit of marine algae, most of which would be covered by the high water.)

The magnificent ebb tide allows me to not only gather seaweeds attached to rocks along the beach, but also to get within arm's length of those that are normally submerged. If there is such a thing as a one-man feeding frenzy, I am it. I stumble among the rocks and through the tide pools, looking for specimens that are healthy and intact. I must work fast, because in Maine the flood tide occurs with a vengeance. I recall one time when my then-eight-year-old son was wandering among rocks that were, at that moment, exposed, while I ambled in the tide pools higher on the beach. The next thing I knew he was screaming for me. I looked up and there he was, an island, surrounded by the swirling, inbound tide. There was no choice but to remove shoes and socks and wade out to retrieve him, and that water was *cold*.

The reason seaweeds cling to rocks is to keep from being washed away by waves and tidal flow. If you grab hold of a seaweed and gently lift it, you'll find its attachment point—a usually broad-based, sometimes fingerlike, structure called a "holdfast" (remember: seaweeds, being algae, have no roots), which secures the seaweed to some firm surface, such as a rock or a shell. The sedentary nature of the vast majority of seaweeds means that they provide valuable habitat (food and shelter) for scads of other creatures: crabs, snails, juvenile fishes, marine worms. For this reason, I sample modestly, taking only what I need, removing any attached invertebrates I find and resettling them under a neighboring plant.

There are, incidentally, some unattached, floating seaweeds. For example, the sargassum weed that occurs in vast fields in the Caribbean gives the Sargasso Sea its name. I have long been enamored of a poem by Henry Wadsworth Longfellow, called — what else? — "Seaweed," in which he extols the virtues of what I presume must be sargassum weed. One of his verses:

> Ever drifting, drifting, drifting
> On the shifting
> Currents of the restless main;
> Till in sheltered coves, and reaches
> Of sandy beaches,
> All have found repose again.

But my objects right now are the attached varieties, those I can grab hold of without getting too wet.

My students find it hard to believe that some biologists — called phycologists (they used to be called "algologists," a term I long for, as it is easier to remember and has a blunt aural appeal befitting the matter-of-factness of its subject organisms) — spend their professional lives studying the seaweeds. When I was an undergraduate I learned of a professor who had discovered a completely new species of marine alga. He named it after his wife, calling it *Patricia elegans*. (A decided improvement over a name like *Fucus vesiculosus*.)

I set my buckets aside, sit down on a large rock and take a break. I am surrounded by seaweeds. Before me the tidal channel continues to rush out to sea, steadily exposing the waving tops of a leathery kelp forest. Up beach are the rockweeds, high but, thanks to their slime coat, not quite dry. At my feet are tough sheets of devil's apron, brown and perforated. In the tidepool not five feet from where I am sitting are tufts of green tubeweed and the pinkish, calcareous, delicately branched *Corallina*.

Before I embarked upon this collecting trip I dramatized the effort for my students, portraying it as something of an adventure (recall Frank Morgan at the end of *The Wizard of Oz*, perched to depart for Kansas in his circus balloon, waving his hat to a cheering crowd). In fact, on some of my trips I have gone to heroic lengths to retrieve that perfect specimen. Once, at Schoodic Point, I carefully slipped into a cleft in a sheer granite face right at the water's edge, as storm waves crashed upon the rocky beach, dousing me with spray. I wanted to retrieve a delicately pleated specimen of the red seaweed "laver" (*Porphyra umbilicalis*). My young son stood gaping at me as I strained after the alga, managing to seize it in my fingertips and scramble from the cleft just as a massive wave exploded at my heels. (When I recount this story to dinner guests, my son, now a teenager, rolls his eyes and declaims, "Oh, Dad, gimme a break!")

Earlier in the course I had primed my students for their first informed contact with seaweeds by telling them some amazing facts about the plants. For example, a single blade of giant kelp can grow to two hundred feet. The floating sargassum weed is where American eels meet for anonymous sex. And if they look at the list of ingredients on a carton of good-quality ice cream, they'll see carrageenan, a seaweed extract added as an emulsifier to lend smoothness to the product.

Like anything else in nature, seaweeds are at their best in their native habitat. From the proper vantage point one is able to look down and see them splayed out like angel hair pasta or shifting about like mopheads. In the gentlest current they sway at ease, as if showing off the latest fashions. When I remove them from the water they collapse into slippery, amorphous clumps. But when I drop them into my bucket of seawater, they blossom again, still beautifully alive, but more sedate in the absence of currents.

The grandmother of a friend of mine was a marine biologist in the early twentieth century, when such a career choice could provide a livelihood for few men, let alone women. When she passed away she left her granddaughter a unique and lovely gift from the sea: a set of individually framed seaweeds that she had ever so carefully lifted from the water on sheets of paper so as to preserve some semblance of their glory for posterity. Each specimen was lovingly hand-lettered in the clear and flowing script of a bygone age.

My students don't realize how much they know about the seaweeds already. Before I left for the coast we discussed them in depth. Seaweeds have no roots because they don't need them: they get their nutrients from the surrounding seawater. Other seaweeds, such as *Polysiphonia*, are so-called "epiphytes" — they live out their lives attached only to other seaweeds. Dense forests of seaweed provide refuge for the juvenile lobster — a mainstay of Maine's economy. Even seaweeds forming rotting strand lines on the beach provide both habitat and food for myriad small invertebrates.

The incoming tide augurs the end of my collecting trip. In my bucket I have fifteen different species. Not bad for an hour's work. But my fingers and the tip of my nose are cold, as are my toes. I pack up my things and begin the drive back to school. When I arrive I will fill fifteen finger bowls with cold, clear seawater and reverentially transfer a seaweed into each one.

When my students enter the laboratory they will set to work, touching, examining, sketching. I feel as if I have prepared a feast for them, and I will stand on the threshold and watch them with deep satisfaction as something that was ill thought of, or even un-thought of, gradually becomes extraordinary for them. ⚶

✡ ✡ ✡ ✡ ✡ ✡ ✡ ✡ ✡ ✡ ✡ ✡ ✡ ✡ ✡ ✡ ✡

through a lens. brightly.

The microscope has been extolled as the most important invention in the history of biology, and I don't dispute this. Of the fourteen weekly laboratory exercises I schedule for my introductory biology course, the use of the microscope is the one I always look forward to with the greatest sense of anticipation, because there is usually one student who is so captivated by the experience that his or her curious mind becomes a hungry one, as if, like a specimen on a slide, it has also been illuminated.

The microscope was invented in the Netherlands in the sixteenth century, and it boggles me to consider that it was not turned to biological materials in any significant way until a hundred years later. It was left to the brilliant, restless, melancholic Englishman Robert Hooke to publish a collection of observations called the *Micrographia* — the first serious work of biological microscopy, and biology has never been the same since.

It's easy to follow in Hooke's footsteps in the undergraduate laboratory because cells of all kinds are exceedingly easy to gather. An onion will yield a limitless supply of plant cells that, properly prepared for observation, resemble a brick wall. A drop of water from a drainage ditch sets the mind spinning with countless single-celled organisms that glide and swarm without cease. One small, delicate, translucent leaf of the freshwater plant *Elodea* shows cells packed with tiny green bodies called chloroplasts — the seats of photosynthesis — that circulate in the cytoplasmic current, faster and faster as one increases the light. In fact, when I was a high schooler I was told that they stream counterclockwise in the northern hemisphere and clockwise in the southern. Although I have long since been disabused of this notion, I have never been able to shake the hankering to take a trip Down Under to see for myself.

But what about animal cells? As my students stand gathered about my desk, I explain that they will harvest these from their own bodies. Then I allow the silence to fester and swell as they wonder how and precisely from where they will glean these cells.

The most easily accessible place is the lining of the mouth. The moist membranes of the inside of the cheeks are constantly shedding thin, flakelike epidermal cells. It's a way of renewing that delicate stratum after we assault it with caustic things like Pepsi, vinegar, hot foods, and jalapeña peppers—the sooner the body gets rid of these damaged cells, the better. We swallow—or spit out—countless numbers of them every day. It would be a shame not to take advantage of the windfall in the biology laboratory. The process is painless. A couple of gentle scrapes with the flat side of a toothpick does it. Then it's just a matter of stirring the cells in a drop of water on a slide, adding a bit of iodine stain to render them visible, and mounting the slide on the stage of the microscope.

I have never had a student who wasn't able to make an exemplary preparation of cheek cells. And it's the rare student who isn't pleased, or even elated, by the sight. They look like soggy cornflakes. But their salient feature is the perfect nucleus that occupies the center of these cells. On one occasion I leaned over a student's shoulder and whispered, "Just think. That nucleus has all of your genes. We could take that nucleus and make a copy of you. A clone. Just think."

(I've often wondered if that student hesitated to rinse off the slide after he had completed his observations.)

I was given a microscope when I was seven, and promptly used it to look at my spit. Considering my early exposure to the instrument, it is always slightly jarring to see how many of my college-age students have never used a microscope. Rather than the child's élan, they tend to bring apprehension to their first interaction with the scope, regarding it as being as complicated as the flight panel of an aircraft.

My students' inexperience has led to some interesting moments. There was the time one of my young jocks took his first glance through the scope and exclaimed, "Oh, my God! Worms! Hundreds of them!" (He had pressed his eye too close to the lens and was observing his own lashes.)

Then there was the student who lamented that not one of her cheek cells had a nucleus. When I took a peek at her slide, I saw a sea of red blood cells (red blood cells do not have nuclei). Instead of gently scraping the inside of her cheek, she had used the toothpick as a lance, breaking who knows how many capillaries.

Another young man showed me his slide, which he had prepared just after lunch. My response: "You had pizza, didn't you?"

Animal cells, plant cells, chloroplasts, amoebas, paramecia, bacteria, diatoms, human hairs . . . all of these have appeared upon the stages of my students' microscopes. For some, they were objects of delight. Others were bamboozled by what they were looking at. And yet others found the experience as electrifying as doing the dishes.

But then, as I mentioned at the outset, there are those who become captivated by the world of the microscope. It's as if they've established a psychic link with the instrument and simply cannot pull themselves away. I get one, maybe two of these students per year. They're recognizable by the quiet, careful way they go about their work, and their protracted hovering over each specimen, as if reluctant to take leave of a true love. Then, when the class period ends, they linger at their places, solitary islands of earnest intent.

Chris exemplified this type of student, the one whose face becomes radiant upon seeing his first cell; the one who asks where he can buy a scope; the one who decouples himself from the rest of the class because he has circumscribed a world of his own, by which he becomes consumed.

Chris was a late teen, strikingly handsome. There wasn't a female student in the class who could keep her eyes off him. He wasn't brilliant, but he was above average academically and worked hard for his grades. It brought a smile to my face that he seemed oblivious to the attentions of the womenfolk, even when they jockeyed to be his partner in lab.

As for his relationship to the microscope, I knew exactly what was going on. It was the same thing that had happened to me when I looked at my spit at the age of seven. I can still remember thinking, "So *this* is what science is." And I never stopped peering through lenses.

Chris, clearly, had had a similar epiphany. As soon as he turned on the illuminator of his scope and took his first gander at a cell—his own cheek cell—he was hooked. The females never had a chance after that, because Diamond Lil had come to town and had wrapped Chris around her little finger.

He wanted to know everything there was to know about the microscope, so I started him on some historical references. Then I instructed him in the finer points of microscopy (one can easily teach a semester-long course on microscopy; what is taught in introductory biology courses is no more than a fleeting gloss, in which students are taught how to focus on a specimen while the instructor scrambles from desk to desk, repeating, ad nauseum, "No, that's not a cell; it's an air bubble!")

I gave Chris all the time he asked for, between classes and at the end of the day. I taught him how to use a microtome to cut specimens thin enough for light to pass through. In this way we reproduced Hooke's seminal observation of cork, which had prompted this description: "I no sooner observed these (which were indeed the first microscopical pores I ever saw) . . . but me thought I had with the discovery of them, presently hinted to me the true and understandable reason of all the Cork in the world . . ."

All the cork in the world. Hooke was making a leap here, extrapolating his humble observation to a wider truth: that cells were present not only in his specimen, but in all cork, be it in London, Lisbon, or Trenton, New Jersey. Scientists many years later would extend this reasoning to make an assertion about all living things, both plant and animal, through their formulation of the Cell Theory.

I discussed Hooke and some of the early microscopists with Chris, and he ate it all up. The crossing of our paths over such an esoteric interest was pure serendipity. Some people are born musicians, mathematicians, or bricklayers, but compared with microscopy these opportunities are ubiquitous: we're marinated in music, numbers, and masonry. I wondered what would have tickled Chris's fancy if he had not stumbled upon microscopy.

His interest was no flash in the pan. I taught him how to make his own slides and he went about it with the zealousness of the convert to a new religion. Week upon week he approached me with his handiwork, and what he created was so exquisite that even now, as I write this, I can feel the hairs stand up on the back of my neck. He had made slides of his own blood (differentially staining the red and white cells), the algae from his home aquarium, bacteria from his mouth, the wing of a fruit fly, and a lovely comparative slide of a brown, blond, and red human hair, demonstrating the relative thickness of each. (Blond hairs are the finest.) Within a couple of months he had an impressive slide collection that would easily have netted him an "A" in a course on microtechnique.

Microscopy became a conduit for an ongoing conversation between us. I learned a lot about Chris, as if our relationship were itself a lens into his life. His drug-addicted father had run off when he was very young, and he was raised by what he described as his "frantic" mother, who once pulled a gun on him for reasons I have forgotten. He had been in a juvenile detention facility, stolen a car or two, and gone through a period when, as he put it, he was never un-stoned. So what had happened to make him a serious student? Well, as he told it to me, he wasn't. "I'm doing average in my other courses," he confided one day as he worked at his microscope. "But this course . . ." he said, his voice trailing away. He didn't need to say anything else. Who isn't familiar with the truism that we are good at the things we love?

In the interim, Chris continued to read the history of microscopy. One day, when I had him examining prepared slides of nerve cells, which look like little starbursts, he mentioned early biologists who believed there was a little person wrapped up inside their own sperm.

"Yes," I corroborated. "The homunculus."

Chris grew pensive. And then, whispering, as if he were being indiscreet, "Could I see my own sperm?"

His question took me off guard. I hesitated, and then asked, "Do you mean, is it possible to, or that you want to?"

"Want."

Well, why not? I let him take a microscope home and slept soundly that night, knowing I had done my bit for American education. But perhaps the confrontation with his genetic legacy was too much for Chris. He dropped out of school and stayed in sporadic touch before disappearing into the American West. A terrible shame. He was a damn fine microscopist, and that's something no one will ever be able to take from him. In the meantime, I have a new student, very promising. At the moment she's examining the microanatomy of the sponge, *Grantia asconoides*.

For the fourth time. ♣

methodologies

✳ ✳ ✳ ✳ ✳ ✳ ✳ ✳ ✳ ✳ ✳ ✳ ✳ ✳ ✳ ✳ ✳

the bell jar

Once, years ago, when I was teaching a section in my human biology course on what is knowable and whether absolute knowledge is possible, I made reference to Einstein, who early on met with formidable skepticism about his theory of relativity. Then I cross-referenced Galileo, who suffered drastic consequences for an idea (the earth revolves around the sun) that directly contradicted the accepted wisdom of the time (that the earth was the center of the solar system).

My students, for the most part, were familiar with the names Einstein and Galileo, but around these points of light the area of darkness was vast, as evidenced by the hand that went up with the following comment/question: "I don't understand. Why didn't Einstein and Galileo just get together and join forces to fight the people who were against them?"

If anything is missing from undergraduate science teaching, it is a historical context. Science is rife with concepts, processes, and (unpronounceable) terminology that have, over the years, driven masses of potential science majors to the warmer and more navigable waters of the college of education.

Let's face it, science has its own language and must have its own language, for two reasons: one, it describes very specific, complex, and esoteric processes; and two, science, being a global pursuit, benefits from a vocabulary that transcends international boundaries. (*Felis domesticus* is *Felis domesticus* whether the kitty cat is romping about a front yard in Passaic, New Jersey, or reclining on a carpet in the Casbah.)

But it is also fair to say that one can get hung up on the vocabulary, the language, of science, to the point where the path of least resistance is to abandon it, embracing, instead, the staid predictability of a business curriculum, where everything has a welcome habit of adding up.

This is where history comes in. Language only works well when it is, somehow, tied together. When we speak, we don't simply emit random words—we line them up in meaningful sentences. And this is exactly the problem with traditional approaches to science teaching: students are tasked with memorizing batteries of disjointed terms and concepts that don't seem to bear upon one another. A little history would provide a narrative that would have some impact and, like any good story, make sense.

Let's talk about the cell. Students in beginning biology courses are normally given a list of structures and functions—nucleus: control center; ribosomes: make RNA; Golgi apparatus: packages proteins, etc.

It is plain that a professor's simply enumerating such a list is not really teaching, but dictation. And the student's ability to memorize the list and reproduce it when prompted by a test is not really learning, but, with apologies to Pavlov, mental salivation.

Perhaps this is one reason why the concept of evolution is a recurring hot potato in American schools. When stated as a factoid ("Humans are descended from lower orders of animals," or something similar) without preamble or some discussion of how the concept, well, evolved over time, I can see where it might strike some students as offensive or wrong-headed, because it would seem to turn everything they know about "Creation" on its noggin.

But what if natural selection—the most well established and widely supported theory of evolution—were taught as part of a continuum of historical thought by famous personalities on how living things came to be and how they have changed over time? Then the conversation might begin with Aristotle, who believed—rightly, most scientists now concur—that all life originated in the sea. From there the individuals who dealt with evolution (before the term even existed) can be lined up like a string of pearls, detailing a truly human grasping after the truth of the matter.

When Darwin is presented to students at first blush as the "father of evolution" or some other such simplification, this does justice to neither Darwin nor the concept at stake. The problem is that, by tossing Darwin out like a live grenade, it does two harms: it labels a man a prophet, and it disrespects science as a process, frequently slow and agonizing, that sometimes spawns individuals—in this case, Charles Darwin—who attempt to make some sense of things for the rest of us.

Look, before Darwin, people weren't stupid. Through the ages, many had suspected that the earth must be older than the Bible seemed to indicate. The problem was that to voice any idea that opposed biblical teachings risked dire consequences, sometimes to the point of death. Is it any wonder that time and tide had to wait for social conditions that would tolerate some free-dom of opinion in the matter?

Until the eighteenth century, the conventional wisdom was that the earth was about six thousand years old, give or take a century or two. It is simply amazing how much staying power this idea has, even today. But reasonable people had spoken up to question such bunk long before. The French naturalist Georges Buffon wrote forty-four volumes of natural history in the mid-eighteenth century. In the course of his labors he suggested — in contravention of Holy Writ — that the earth was probably about one hundred thousand years old. This was a brave and foolhardy assertion during the tumult of the French Revolution, which, in fact, claimed Buffon's life. But the die had been cast, and scien-tists had at last been freed to pursue a more dispassionate exam-ination of earth's history from the standpoint of geology rather than Genesis.

During this same period, perhaps a little later, another French-man, Georges Cuvier, was the contradiction that Buffon was not. Buffon had been a scientist to the core, a materialist who applied consistent principles of scientific observation and deduction to the geological history of the planet. Cuvier, by contrast, was an avid anti-evolutionist who nevertheless made a startling and rev-olutionary observation about fossils: he characterized them as the remains of once-living creatures.

Why should this be so remarkable? Because, in Cuvier's time, fossils were thought to be either unusual rock formations or a sort of divine practical joke devised by the Creator for our amuse-ment. In short, fossils were not looked upon as a threat to peo-ple's self-image of human beings as the centerpiece of Creation. Some were held in so little estimation that, instead of being stud-ied, they were used for mundane purposes, such as doorstops.

It's clear what's happening here. Buffon and Cuvier had opened the window of understanding a little bit. This made some — all right, many — people uncomfortable, but it is the job of politicians, not scientists, to tell people what they want to hear.

If nothing else, these two Frenchmen planted two very important words in the minds of those willing to listen: "what if?"

What if the world is not young, but rather immensely old?

What if living things have changed over time?

What if fossils are the actual remains of strange creatures that once roamed the earth?

Science, in other words, is a slippery slope of one question leading to another, but in contrast to other slippery slopes, its trajectory tends upwards.

The French were really on a roll when it came to formulating theories about the natural world. To this end, it was yet another Frenchman, Jean Baptiste LaMarck, who gave us the first truly systematic theory of evolution, one that served as preamble to Darwin's theory of natural selection.

LaMarck was a naturalist who lived from 1744 to 1829. To him, it seemed clear that living things must have changed. The example most often cited is the giraffe. In LaMarck's eyes, the giraffe could not have always had a long neck. Rather, its ancestors must have had short necks, which, to LaMarck, seemed more "natural." So what happened? Well, according to LaMarck, these short-necked ancestors ate grass and shrubs. But as this food supply was depleted, they had to turn to leaves in the trees. So they stretched their necks and, *within the course of their lifetimes*, their necks got longer. They then proceeded to give birth to long-necked babies.

See the problem? What LaMarck was saying, in essence, was that if you cut off a mouse's tail its babies will be tailless. He called this the Theory of Evolution by Acquired Characteristics. For LaMarck, physical change could be willed by the individual organism, and passed to its offspring. Very interesting, but very wrong.

Enter Charles Darwin. LaMarck died when Darwin was twenty years old. The younger man was very much aware of LaMarck's work and indeed was deeply influenced by it. But Darwin's idea was different in two radical ways: one, he believed that physical changes were slow, taking place over thousands or millions of years; and two, he asserted that it was the entire species population, and not the individual organism, that evolved. He presented his great idea in his book, *On the Origin of Species by Means of Natural Selection*, the first edition of which was sold out before it hit the stands. It caused an uproar, whose echoes are still reverberating. Darwin was mercilessly vilified by the press of his time, and there is not one photograph of this rather reclusive hypochondriac with a smile on his face.

The problem with the American hubbub over evolution is that Darwin is looked upon as the last word in evolution, as if scientists, for the past one hundred and fifty years, have rested upon the laurels of Darwin's work. This is tragically untrue. Darwin has always been intensely studied, criticized, and elaborated upon. His work, in other words, was never an endpoint, but rather a springboard for further investigation. Darwin, in short, has been the poster child deluxe for how science really operates: it is the product of persistent, focused, stop-and-go research by human beings, most of whom are no smarter than you or me. They simply burn with a passion for a specific problem, in the same way that a teenager might obsess over customizing an engine to the point where he eventually learns a great deal and is able to teach others.

I was driving this very point home one day during a lecture on evolution. I had placed a framed portrait of Darwin on the upper edge of the blackboard, as a sort of inspiring focal point. After describing the mechanics of natural selection, I assured my students that "while Darwin's theory of evolution by natural selection is believed by the great majority of scientists to be true in the main, not everyone agrees with all its details." As I said this, I rapped on the board for emphasis and the portrait fell — crack! — on my head. The students roared. I recouped my grace by telling them that even when a scientist reaches out from the grave, we must persist in challenging him.

I believe that a course in the history of science should be part of the curriculum for any science major. Or, alternatively, all science courses should integrate science history by describing the struggles, contributions, virtues, and shortcomings of the individuals involved. It's one thing to state, dryly, that radium was discovered by Marie and Pierre Curie in 1898. But how much more engaging—and moving—it is to learn that these two scientists did their work in a damp and drafty Parisian warehouse, and that they used to visit their speck of luminous metal on warm summer evenings, and that Marie Curie died of a cancer most likely brought on by exposure to a radioactive substance whose power, and toxicity, science had not yet come to understand.

In a similar way Darwin can be defanged. Presented point blank as that evolution guy, he brings to the minds of the uninformed the famous cartoon image of the ape with the head of the scientist. But when one learns that his studies in medicine and theology didn't amount to anything, and that his father once remarked that he was "good for nothing besides shooting and rat catching," we see someone rife with self-doubt and personal failings. And when we read the very last paragraph of *The Origin of Species*, the charge that Darwin was Godless is shown to be false:

> There is grandeur in this view of life with its several powers, having been originally breathed by the Creator into a few forms or into one; and that, while this planet has gone circling on according to the fixed law of gravity, from so simple a beginning endless forms most beautiful and most wonderful have been, and are being evolved.

Once we understand the scientists, it leads, ideally, to curiosity about what drove them, and why their ideas matter today. ⚶

※ ※ ※ ※ ※ ※ ※ ※ ※ ※ ※ ※ ※ ※ ※ ※ ※

how i youtubed my biology course

I've been a latecomer to many aspects of the electronic revolution. I was late getting into computers, late getting a high-speed connection, and late getting a cell phone. In this last matter, I bought the cheapest phone I could find, with the cheapest plan. I carried this phone for years, a thick, bulky thing with a brick-size vibrating battery. The rig looked like something the Soviet Union might have produced at the height of the Cold War.

Needless to say, I was a latecomer to YouTube. I had heard of it, but in the same way people have heard of Greenland: I knew it existed, but beyond that, almost nothing. Despite this, I kept an open ear when I heard my students exulting over this or that YouTube video. At first, I didn't know what they were talking about, but everything associated with YouTube seemed to be funny. At least to them: amateur musicians who couldn't sing, narcoleptic dogs, foul-mouthed toddlers, animal tricks, practical jokes, and farting. If this was what YouTube was all about, I wasn't missing anything.

And then, one evening, I found my ten-year-old son riveted to the computer. I tactfully passed behind him and looked over his shoulder. He was watching a YouTube video on skateboard maintenance. I'm not a skateboarder, and the clip was very unprofessional, but the kid doing the explaining was earnest and knowledgeable. At that moment, although I wasn't yet aware of it, a seed was planted.

I still didn't have much contact with YouTube in the ensuing weeks. But one day, as I was organizing materials for a lecture on DNA, I panicked when I couldn't find the well-worn video I used to illustrate the workings of this molecule of life. I had only an hour before class, so there was no possibility of ordering another video or finding a library that might have it. And then, well, why not give it a try? I went to YouTube and did a search for "DNA." I was rewarded with a cornucopia of video clips on the subject. With my lecture fast approaching, I had nothing to lose. I began to work my way through the videos.

The effort was akin to mining diamonds: a lot of rock had to be chiseled out of the way to access the occasional gem. But gems there were. An investment of twenty minutes at the keyboard rewarded me with three precious clips: DNA structure, DNA replication, and protein synthesis. Exactly what I needed. I bookmarked these and headed for class.

After booting up the computer, I commenced my lecture in the usual fashion, introducing DNA, holding up a model, and discussing James Watson and Francis Crick, the two scientists who worked out its structure back in the 1950s. And then, seamlessly, as if I were an old hand at it, I turned on the projector, clicked the first YouTube videos, and . . . magic. The clip was only one minute and nineteen seconds long, but the author had produced it with utmost care and professionalism. It showed my students all that I wanted them to know about the structure of this molecule, and in a dynamic, clearly presented manner. What's more, it was available to all of them on the Web.

In my years of teaching there have not been many sea-change moments (the last two were the advent of personal computers and the transition from ditto machines and their sweet-smelling spirit fluid to photocopiers). But this YouTube thing was certainly one of them. I was hooked. For me, it was like discovering a new species.

I quickly realized that YouTube was the ticket to rescuing one of my courses that had gone creaky in the joints: marine biology. I taught this course once a year, during the fall semester. One of the major sections involved the marine invertebrates — animals, like jellyfishes and sea urchins, that have no backbone. It's a massive, diverse group of startlingly beautiful creatures. My students had seen few of them either in the wild or in captivity. I tried to make up for this deficiency by passing around specimens that were pickled in formalin or were entombed in blocks of plastic. I even had a dessicated horseshoe crab, brittle as a cracker, which was missing three legs. Seeing and handling these preserved specimens gave the students a sense of the real thing, but such static presentations did not even hint at the beauty and dynamism they radiated in life. After my success with the DNA video, I decided, without hesitation, to YouTube my marine biology course.

I was surprised how quickly this could be done. Sitting by a wood fire at home with my laptop, I went through my list of invertebrate phyla — sponges, corals and relatives, mollusks, arthropods (crustaceans and associates) . . . YouTube had them all covered. Some of the videos were simple, but effective and accurate, homemade jobs, like the one a fellow put together showing him feeding a piece of meat to his pet sea anemone. Another showed a teacher holding a sea cucumber he had just lifted from the shallows. And then there were the breathtaking ones: professionally shot videos of marine creatures in the wild. A massive, bulbous sea cucumber snuffling in the sea bed; a scallop chattering like a set of wind-up false teeth to escape a starfish; a hassock-size, brilliantly colored jellyfish pulsing beneath arctic ice. And on and on, a movable feast of invertebrate diversity. An embarrassment of riches. If anything impeded the selection process it was the sheer volume of awe-inspiring clips, which begged the question, which ones to choose?

Well, choose I did. And present I did. With lowered lights and plenty of popcorn, I initiated the show I had put together for my students. They resonated immediately to the images (after all, this was YouTube!). Needless to say, I could pause the clips to point out or discuss various characteristics of the creatures — halting, for example, a Portuguese man-'o-war as it hauled a fish into its horrific maw. The "oohs" and "ahs" of the class were confirmation that I — or rather, the YouTube images — had engaged them and fired their enthusiasm.

There is a moral here, to wit: it is not difficult to revise a course, especially in this age of unlimited access to information. This brave new world of instructional technology renders quaint the image of the senior professor holding yellowed notes as fragile as a Dead Sea Scroll, squinting through bifocals to make out details he had penned when Eisenhower was president. Revising a course today does not require that one attend a symposium, hobnob with one's fellow wizards, or otherwise dedicate a year's sabbatical to rewriting, from scratch, an entire syllabus. It's possible to retain core information but cast it in a new and improved light, as I did by applying YouTube to my marine biology course.

Technology is especially important when one is teaching cutting-edge material. Every spring I teach a course in the biology of cancer, an area in which I subscribe to a steady flow of Internet information, which is constantly being generated, in an almost frantic fashion, by the work of innumerable research laboratories. Here, too, I have integrated YouTube into my course. Who would have guessed that the same entity that hosts video clips on vomiting frat boys and female mud wrestlers would also include well-made, accurate, and sophisticated information on cancer genes, tumor-killing viruses, and the fast-tracking of cancer drugs?

Which brings me to Krista. Her mind was oil to my marine biology course's water: one repelled the other. She fascinated me because even the most concrete, fundamental concepts seemed to bamboozle her. And yet, during our conversations, I perceived real intelligence. I soon concluded that she came to the course with powerful assumptions about its difficulty, and about her inability to learn science to any degree. Whenever she sat down to a test I could sense her apprehension, which made me feel that I was somehow punishing her. The results were invariably poor. She even, on one test, failed to answer several true or false questions because, as she later told me, she didn't want to risk being wrong.

As an experiment, I decided to YouTube her. It was an effort to salvage a student and to instill in her some degree of confidence that she could succeed. I put her on a separate track of instruction, or rather, self-instruction. It took a little time and elbow grease on my part, but I spent an evening identifying and bookmarking video clips on YouTube. The topic was genetics. I found pieces on Gregor Mendel, the father of genetics, as well as chromosomes and genes, and how traits were transmitted. I also drew up some worksheets for Krista, so that she would have some product of her labors. "Within the next three weeks," I directed her, "I want you to complete these worksheets. Then I want you to sit down with me for a discussion of the material." I scrupulously avoided the word "test." She agreed, and disappeared into the ether for that period. Every so often I received an e-mail from her, asking for clarification of this or that point, which I was happy to provide.

In the interim, of course, I continued to teach the rest of my class in the traditional manner: lecture, laboratory, handouts, quizzes, tests. But Krista was always on my mind, and her occasional e-mails told me that she was still out there, on a tether, working her way through the material. She e-mailed me her worksheets as attachments, which I dutifully examined, corrected, and commented on, satisfied that she was, in actuality, making good use of her time. And then, after the three weeks were up, came the tes . . . er, reckoning.

"You did well on your worksheets," was my first comment as Krista took a seat opposite me in my office. "Now let's have a little chat." I think that was the word that put her at ease. Chat. I began to talk about DNA and genes the way one might broach the topic of the weather. Krista needed a little prodding to get started, but she soon found her groove and actually put sentences together into ideas that indicated a decent degree of understanding. Her insights were not brilliant by any measure, but she was reasonably conversant in the subject matter. The thing was, she was the only one of my students about whom I could actually say this, because, testing the other students the way I did, I really didn't know how fluent their comprehension was. If I ran into them at an elegant dinner party and commented, "Isn't that deoxyribonucleic acid something?" I have no idea what kind of response I'd get. But with Krista I could honestly say, "She knows what she's talking about."

Last night I had a dream that YouTube had all but replaced me in the classroom. I had been relegated to the role of a conduit, conveying video clips to my students the way a downspout funnels water. There they sat, before their computers, clicking away, nodding, and then typing up their responses. My entire course—lecture, laboratory, discussion questions—was now being delivered by video clips of the most diverse and wondrous natures, segregated by topic. It was an ebb of images followed by a flow of finished work back to me. And then the dream ended.

How many in history have been inspired by such visions? Not long ago I would have considered the whole video clip business tawdry, and even now there is something of the dirty fingernail about it, because it seems too easy. But I have become intrigued by such possibilities and am actually considering the creation of an entire biology course based on YouTube, with me as the arbiter of acceptable results and good taste. I think there are real possibilities here, and for the first time in my professional life, I feel that I just might be at the leading edge of a unique wave. ⚜

how to study

Biology—or any science, for that matter—is a rich stew of the factual, the conceptual, and the theoretical. On the one hand, there is the immense overhead of terminology, discoveries, dates, and personalities. On the other are the intricate, and daunting, themes of evolution, cell physiology, and genetics, to name only a few. In short, biology, unlike history or English composition, is truly an alien world with its own — and for the student, sometimes unbreathable — atmosphere. My impression is that, more than with any other introductory courses — including dreaded math — beginning students fall like flies from the sciences because they are overwhelmed with anxiety about how they will come to terms with a language as unfamiliar to them as Hottentot.

In my introductory biology class, I try to bear this in mind. On the very first day I ask, "Is there anyone here who has never had a biology course?" Several hands go up. My second question: "Is there anyone here who is afraid of biology?" A few more hands, mostly in the back row. My response: "I accept the challenge."

There is one powerful difference between the biology major and the non-major. The former has, arguably, learned how to study biology. The latter has almost no idea. What I propose to do here is to review how non-majors *do* study, and then suggest how they *should* study.

Through years of instruction, I have learned which concepts my students invariably have difficulty with. Semester upon semester, they make the same mistakes about the same material. My conclusion, based on careful observation and interviews, is that they make the same mistakes because most students study the exact same way, even as they continue to do poorly.

Whenever I have a student who just doesn't "get it" and whose test grades remain in the basement, I take that student aside and, after ascertaining that there are no personal crises or other issues to account for his or her lackluster performance, I ask a simple question: "How do you study?"

Invariably, they tell me that they go home and read their notes. This, I point out, is the worst way to study. Reading notes and expecting to recall details is like taking one look at a roadmap to a remote destination and expecting to recall every junction and turn. If we were allowed to use roadmaps only before — but not during—a trip, would we examine them any differently? I think so.

Let's talk about Neil, a tall, wiry, articulate student who was not doing well in my course (although I depended upon him to occasionally lighten the mood with his pointed sense of humor). I looked at him as he draped his frame over the arms of the "hot seat" in my office. After we agreed that he was doing poorly, I asked him, "How do you study?"

"Well," he began, sitting up as if preparing to say something momentous, "I go home, take out my notebook, and read."

"So," I countered, "if you read something like, 'the terebellid polychaete has uncinial tori,' you need only see this once to be able to recall it on a test?"

Neil blinked at me. "Could you repeat that?"

Exactly.

Someday someone will realize that studying an academic subject is like practicing music. When a student is presented with a new piece to play on his clarinet, he goes at it slowly at first, moving through the music until he comes to a passage that gives him trouble. So he slows down, placing each finger upon its appointed key or tone hole with the utmost deliberation. Over and over. Finally, persistence pays off, and "muscle memory" takes over. The piece has been internalized and the music teacher weeps tears of joy.

Granted, looking at pages of biology notes is not as gratifying as practicing Beethoven and imagining the day when it will translate into angelic tones from one's instrument. Therefore, it takes extra fortitude and drive to practice one's classroom notes. Creative approaches should be productive, make the time pass, and be enjoyable. Here are some strategies guaranteed to improve one's grades:

One. Keep two notebooks—one for class and another that stays home. Since the notes that students take in class are created "on the run," they tend to be sloppy and, in many cases, unintelligible. That's where the second notebook comes in. It's important that the student take the classroom notebook home and, that very night—at the kitchen table, bathed in a soft pool of light, with a cup of hot cocoa at hand—transcribe, ever so carefully, those classroom notes into the second notebook. And here's the important part: any time the student comes to a term or concept that he does not understand, he should underline or circle it in red, then look it up or have the professor explain it the next day. What the student winds up with is a clean, neat, legible notebook that leaves no questions unanswered.

Two. Looking at one's notes is simply an exercise in recognizing familiar information that may or may not make sense. Simply reading one's notes is akin to looking at a building and saying, "Yes, this is architecture," and leaving it at that. One must now make the leap to *generating* correct information. How is this done? By finding a competent study partner, perhaps two (any more than two is not a study group; it's a party).

Here's the set-up. Let's say there are two of you sitting at a table, across from one another (*avec* soft light, cocoa, and notebooks). One person opens his or her notebook and asks the other person three questions while this second person's notebook is closed. If the interrogee answers the questions correctly, swell; but the questioner puts a red mark next to any question that is not answered in a satisfactory manner. That question will be revisited over and over (practice!) until it is correctly and fully answered. Then the roles are reversed—the questioner becomes the questioned. This goes on until all the notes have been covered (but no longer than two hours at a sitting or until the cocoa runs out). What one accomplishes is the transference of the information from paper to brain, to the point where one can finally discuss the material without benefit of having to refer to one's notes. That's real learning.

Three. Do not memorize the professor's definitions verbatim. Come up with your own. In my classroom, I resist, as much as possible, the temptation to give pat definitions. I try to explain the terms and give relevant examples. Invariably, however, a student will ask, "Can you give me a definition for that?" My response, uttered gently, is usually, "No. Try to understand what this term means, and then write your own definition."

The point is that it is difficult to recall a phalanx of definitions as issued by the teacher, because the student becomes obsessed with memorizing every word exactly as it was spoken. I would much rather have them become obsessed with the concept itself. Here's an example: Natural Selection. Definition: "In any species population there exist physical and behavioral differences called variations. Those individuals with variations that better suit them to their environment have the best chance of surviving to pass on their superior characteristics to their offspring."

Whew!

Who on earth wants to memorize that? Even if one succeeds, one has only proven that one can memorize. But what if one doesn't succeed? What if the student, at test time, gets flustered and forgets a word or two? Anxiety sets in, pressure builds, the entire definition is forgotten, the test is a disaster, and working the drive-in window at Burger King once again extends its appeal.

However, what if the student listens in class to the point where he or she gains a real understanding of natural selection and can write a unique and accurate definition? Here's one I gleaned from a student test:

> Natural Selection deals with populations of individuals of the same species. Some are faster, smarter, stronger, or more beautiful than others. These have an advantage in the fight to survive. They have a better chance of living to reproduce and make babies with these superior traits. Over time, the whole species population will change because of this.

Bravo. Bravissimo. I couldn't have said it better myself (well, yes, I could have, but why quarrel with success?).

Four. Use flashcards, if you think they will help, but learn to use them the right way.

For most students, flash cards mean putting a term on one side and a definition on the other. Once again, they wind up as participants in a Pavlovian exercise in which the term, over time, simply cues a response. Eventually, one term even cues their recollection of the next one, until, with eyes glazed over, the student is reciting a rosary of flash cards while staring vacantly into the void.

So what's the right way to employ this study device? For starters, the flashcards have to be used both frontwards and backwards. In other words, read the terms first and then flip the cards to confirm one's knowledge of the definitions (which, of course, are the student's, and not the instructor's). Then turn the pile over and read the definitions to see if one can come up with the terms they refer to. Then — leap of faith — shuffle the cards and start over again. (This is meant to disrupt the Pavlov Effect of one card's prompting recall of the contents of the next.)

Five. Spelling counts. (Believe it or not.) Why? Because when one takes the time to spell something correctly — especially an elusive scientific term — one is forced to think slowly and carefully.

Spelling is the disposable discipline, the one that teachers tend to de-emphasize. I have never met a professor who felt that spelling was in any way important. This is a venial sin. Perhaps mortal. To say that spelling doesn't matter is to say that the term "proboscis" is just as acceptable when it is spelled "poboskis." If one cannot spell, one cannot use a dictionary, one cannot write, one may confuse "curare" and "calamine" with fatal results.

How does one go about learning to spell correctly? Here's how: make a list of accurately spelled terms from one's notes or the text. Then read the list onto a tape or other recording device. Take out a blank sheet of paper and play back the tape. Repeat, over and over, until you can write out every term correctly. It's a path to literacy, it will make you proud of yourself, and you will feel more confident and knowledgeable as a result of your command of correctly spelled terminology.

Last. The student must learn to overstudy. There is a wonderful—if frightening—line from the movie "The Untouchables," where Sean Connery, a beat cop, is telling Kevin Costner, playing Eliot Ness, how to deal with the mob. In his best Chicago accent, Connery asserts, "They pull a knife, you pull a gun. He sends one of yours to the hospital, you send one of his to the morgue." Likewise, if you think, prior to a test, that you can cover your notes in one hour, study for two. If you think it will take two, put in three. Every night. Commence this process of repetition (practice!) one week before the test, but—leap of faith again—don't study at all the night before the test. Trust me. After all that hard work, give the brain just one evening of respite to sort it all out and deposit the information into the proper slots.

All of this is a lot of advice. But, taken together, it will work. Will it make an "A" student out of a failing student? Probably not (but who knows?). But one last point needs to be made: colleges and universities call their subject areas "disciplines" for a reason, because that's what it takes to master them. ✿

✿ ✿ ✿ ✿ ✿ ✿ ✿ ✿ ✿ ✿ ✿ ✿ ✿ ✿ ✿ ✿ ✿
the truth is in the tape

Despite all my years of college teaching, and despite knowing that I should know better, I still harbor the illusion of being able to get through to all of my students. In fact, I once had a dream in which, on the last day of class, I wandered among the desks, dispensing A's from a basket to eager, interested souls, as rewards for their hard work, diligence, and mastery of introductory biology.

And then—poof!—I awoke. Such are the things, Horatio, that I dream of in my philosophy.

On a more realistic note, I have spent many, many nights at the kitchen table, making my way through seemingly endless piles of student papers. Some of the work was fairly competent and required that I write only occasional, modest glosses in the margins. But much of it was, to be blunt, disastrous, evoking such detailed, lengthy comments from me that the margins became a dense and all but illegible scrawl of well-intentioned wisdom. Through it all, as I critiqued syntax, grammar, content, and style, I was haunted by one nagging question: Will the students read it? This fear was highlighted one day when, shortly after returning my students' assignments, I found one in the wastepaper basket. Unread. Unheeded. Unloved.

Alas, it was too easy for my students to discard corrected work. By and large, they wanted to know only one thing: their grade. In a sense, I understood where they were coming from. Who wants to get a paper back that, like some recovered palimpsest, is overlain with my underlinings, circles, exclamation points, and existential questions such as, "What are you trying to say here?" (I didn't know, and in most cases they didn't know, so the answer lay, more often than not, in the round file.)

I continued to wrestle with this quandary for semesters on end, until one day I noticed a student headed down the hallway with a Walkman (this was quite a few years ago). He looked alert, engaged, and had a mean hitch in his giddy-up as he bopped to the tunes being piped into his brain. Hmmm . . . I thought. That kid knows the truth.

I bided my time until the next semester, when I presented a new grading approach to my students (who were fresh and still unsure of who exactly I was. In other words, they were pliant, and I seized the moment). "Ladies and gentlemen," I announced, and then went on to explain that they would need to hand in their laboratory essays along with a blank cassette tape, on which I would record my comments.

At first they were alarmed, because they feared that they would have to say something on the tape. But I assured them that the process was strictly a one-way street. "I will do all the talking," I said, and then I gave my rationale for this different way of correcting their work, pointing out that it would allow me to make a clearer, more nuanced critique, as well as address each and every one of them in a more personal manner. All they needed to do was listen to the tape and follow along in their essays as I spoke (and, of course, heed my counsel and try to improve their work).

The first batch of papers and accompanying tapes soon arrived. I took them home and, that evening, spread them out on the living room floor, each tape lying in state upon its essay. And then I began the harvest. These were the first papers from this new crop of students, so most were pretty rocky pieces of work. Part of the reason was that, like ants, they were feeling forward, cautiously, with their intellectual and emotional antennae, not exactly sure what I was looking for. With this in mind, I trod softly on these initial papers, laying down some ground rules for myself, to wit: address the student by name; thank him or her for handing the work in on time; and last, even if the paper was simply impossible, say something—anything—positive at the outset, so as to invite the students to pay attention to my comments.

It was a lot of work. I found that, whereas it might take me ten to fifteen minutes to write my remarks in a paper's margins, I spent upwards of twenty on the tape, because my voice could hold out longer than my hand, and I was able to explain things in greater depth verbally, especially when I had some sense that, out of curiosity if nothing else, the students would listen to me.

When I returned the papers and tapes, my students madly paged through the essays, until one young man exclaimed, "Hey, where's the grade?" Er, yes, that was an item I had forgotten to explain. The grade was on the tape, and not necessarily at the very end, so they would have to listen to the tape from the beginning to find out what they got. They took their papers and cassettes and, at the end of class, skulked off to their next labors, not quite sure what they had gotten themselves into.

What did they think? How did it work out? I got an inkling a short while later, when I crossed through the lounge and found five of my students huddled around a little black cassette player. It felt weird to watch people listening to my voice, so I hurried away.

The acid test for my tape idea, however, did not lie in that first batch of essays. It has been said that anyone can poke a piano key and get a clear tone, but one has to poke the second key in just the right way and at just the right moment to get — music. I knew that the mark of the success of the cassette tape approach would lie in whether the second wave of essays was any better than the first; in other words, did the students, after listening to the tapes, apply my advice toward improving the weaknesses in their writing?

I didn't have long to wait. Now that they had survived one round of corrections, an air of increased confidence permeated the class. The next essays looked a little neater, a few students had even placed illustrations on the title page, and, when I sat down to correct them, for the first time a couple of them had ventured to say something on the tape. One commented, "This is fun." Another: "I learned so much by listening to the first tape." A third student had mustered the courage to tell me an endless joke, the punch line of which still eludes me.

These second essays were, on the whole, marginally better than the first. But there was one paper that caught my eye. It was from a kid named Jeff. His initial essay had been nothing short of abysmal. First, it was a physical wreck — poorly formatted on three wrinkled sheets of paper. Second, it was a technical mess — bad spelling, impossible syntax, and a stream-of-consciousness style that elucidated nothing. When I recorded my comments on Jeff's tape, I had to periodically kick myself as a reminder to be kind, because what I really wanted to do was scream. I wound up deciding not to try to win the war of his paper in one fell swoop. Instead, I picked a battle: presentation. "Jeff," I recorded, "the one thing on your next paper I want you to improve is how it looks. I want to see paragraphs, margins, and clean, white, flat paper."

Jeff's next essay rose to the challenge. Content-wise, it was still a lot of gobbledygook, but on the surface it *looked* good. Jeff quickly became my pet project, so on this third paper I decided to amass my troops for a sweeping maneuver against his grammar. Teaching him the rudiments of English on a tape was impossible, but I did offer this advice: "Jeff, before you hand your next paper in, I want you to do two things: one, read it out loud. If it doesn't sound like English, fix it. Second, have somebody else read it, and ask them to circle any sentence they don't understand. Then fix those sentences so that they do understand them."

Like the ebb and flow of the tides, I returned Jeff's essay and tape to him, and a week later his fourth assignment rolled back to me. It looked good. Neat and clean. When I opened it, I saw actual sentences and paragraphs. When I read it, I'd say it was 25 percent better than his previous paper. And so I joined the next battle: writing for understanding. After complimenting Jeff on the improvements he had made, I asked him to begin to think about his audience: "I want you to write your next essay with an imaginary reader in mind. Make believe you are writing it for somebody who has not done this laboratory experiment. This person will learn everything from you, so take him by the hand and lead him through, step-by-step. Take pains to be clear and complete in your comments, so that our imaginary reader does not look up from your work and say, 'Now, what on earth was all this about?'"

A week later, paper number five came in. By now I felt that I was teaching entirely for Jeff's benefit, and I looked forward to his work with a great deal of anticipation. My expectations were rewarded with a pretty competent piece of writing. It was by no means perfect — Jeff was simply out of his depth when trying to explain the theory behind his experiments — but what he did manage to write down was clean, lean, coherent prose, however superficial its level of understanding. When I recorded my comments on his tape, I felt as if I were making a statement for the ages: "Jeff, I couldn't be more pleased with your willingness to edit and improve your work." He had clearly arrived at the point where I could begin to help him fine-tune his writing, targeting the rarified area of style.

In the meantime, I had to remind myself that I had other students as well. I would say that most—perhaps 80 percent— were riding an upward curve as far as their own essays were concerned. I attributed much of this directly to their heeding the counsel of the tapes. Slowly but surely, their papers as a whole were making the transition from loosely written, often careless collections of ideas to well-presented, logical progressions of observations, discussions, and conclusions. I was proud of them and told them so.

As the semester progressed, autumn began to yield to the impending winter. The still-warm September days had turned to cool October, which gave way to the rainy, ambiguous days of November, and then December arrived with its clear inklings of winter: early darkness, chill mornings, and the first snows. All of this created a sense of urgency. My thoughts continued to be with Jeff, who was a pit bull of determination to do well, hanging onto his gentleman's C by dint of his increasingly competent essay work. The thing was, he was within fingernail reach of a B minus, but his last essay needed to be exceptional.

At the end of the semester my students dropped their last laboratory essays into the bin on my desk. Except for Jeff. I looked at him and raised an eyebrow, as we both knew how much was riding on his final piece of writing. He approached me after the test. "Printer problem," he said in his clipped manner. "Can I give it to you after lunch?" I told him to bring it to my office.

Jeff arrived around one o'clock, essay in hand. He held it out to me, lying flat on his upturned palms, like an offering. "I learned a lot from the tapes," he assured me with a sincere heart. "Despite the cold."

"The cold?" I echoed, not sure of his meaning.

That's when I learned how hard Jeff had really worked.

"Yeah," he said. "I don't have my own tape recorder, but there's one in my dad's old truck out in the woods. So at night I go out there, start it up, and sit and listen to the tapes."

The image of Jeff huddled in a pickup, deep in the dark and snow of the Maine woods, listening to my voice, totally unmanned me. If not for the tapes, I might never have known how seriously Jeff took his education. They also allowed me to touch this earnest student in a way my written comments never could. For his part, Jeff's final report was a bang-up job and he got his B minus for the course.

That was fifteen years ago. I'm still doing the tapes, but the service they provide my students pales against the insights they occasionally yield into how truly good-hearted and deserving many of these people are.

In a profession that can too easily become routine, that's an idea that should be cast in bronze, or at least recorded on cassette. ♈

♈ ♈ ♈ ♈ ♈ ♈ ♈ ♈ ♈ ♈ ♈ ♈ ♈ ♈ ♈ ♈ ♈

please hold the morphine

A colleague of mine from a neighboring college once paid me a visit for the sole purpose of expressing his despondency over his inability to teach his students the metric system. "I can't do it anymore," he lamented. "I can't even bring the words, 'there are ten millimeters in a centimeter,' to my lips." But he stopped short of crying.

He had come to the right person. I knew exactly what he was talking about. In the sciences, there are some concepts so fundamental that they simply cannot be dispensed with or glossed over, as they are key to a general and correct understanding of the subject as a whole. But there is also tremendous frustration in teaching such simple concepts. The metric system is one of these. It was developed by Gabriel Mouton, abbot of St. Paul's, Lyon, France, in 1670. Do the foreign origins of this system have anything to do with American resistance to it? Is it any comfort that we are in the company of Myanmar and a few other backwaters that have not adopted it?

Because the metric system is essential to scientific measurements, it must not only be introduced early on, in the primary grades, but thereafter drummed in repeatedly, until its units are as familiar as inches and miles. The problem is that the United States has only grudgingly moved toward the use of this system, even in the sciences, if one can believe such a thing. The result of this dual system (English and metric) can be catastrophic (and embarrassing). In 1999 NASA's $125 million Mars Climate Orbiter was lost because the manufacturer (Lockheed) had used English measurements but NASA transmitted the commands in metric units. The spacecraft is now believed to be orbiting the sun, recording, perhaps, the only weather data possible: hot, very hot.

While elementary school children accept the metric system at face value — the way they accept everything that is new to them — college students who have not been exposed to it, or who have forgotten the little they may have been taught in the early grades, are a different story. There seems to be a defensive wall against learning it, or an assumption that it is astoundingly complicated and therefore hopeless. In my own course, I try to treat the metric system as a language, taking pains to use it in common discourse. When a student is looking at a specimen through a microscope, I ask, "How many micrometers long do you think it is?" When we go outside to set up quadrants in a grassy field for plant population studies, I tell them, "Be sure your quadrants are five meters on a side." And yet I always have the sneaking feeling that they are regarding me as a pretender, or a character from *Star Trek* announcing the distance to a Klingon warship. For my part, I sense that they are surreptitiously converting meters to feet, just to hedge their bets.

"There are ten millimeters in a centimeter," I recite to myself as I stand before my class. "Ten millimeters in a centimeter, ten millimeters in a centimeter . . ." And yet, when I look into their eyes, I'm sure they're repeating to themselves, "There are twenty-five millimeters in an inch . . ." And so I try to give them a solid, useful, immediate sense of the necessity of metric measurements. I direct them to mount a slide of an ameba on their microscopes. Then I tell them to take their rulers and measure the ameba in inches. Of course, this is impossible, and I watch as they insert the rulers under the objective lens of the scope and squint with palpable frustration to measure the tiny organisms against its scale. Inches, of course, are much too large a unit for measuring something too small to be seen with the naked eye. So I tell them to replace the English ruler with a small, transparent metric ruler. Palpable relief. They can see two- or three-millimeter lines; but the ameba still occupies a small fraction of one of these millimeters. The students could estimate what fraction of a millimeter the ameba represents, but this is crude guesswork. Better to use even smaller metric units called micrometers (1000 micrometers = 1 millimeter). Now they can estimate the ameba's size in whole units.

The moral here is that using English units in microscopy is like using a pipe wrench to adjust those little screws on your glasses. Worse, it is like having available to you not only a pipe wrench, but a hammer, chisel, and ripsaw as well. In other words, English measurements are too cumbersome for microscopical and other scientific work. That system is a hodgepodge of tons, pounds, feet, and miles. If students can comprehend such arbitrary units of measurement, surely they can master the logic and simplicity of the metric system, which employs orders of ten: there are ten millimeters in a centimeter, ten centimeters in a decimeter, ten decimeters in a meter, and so on.

I recall once noodling on the Web and finding, of all things, a poem on the metric system extolling its coolness. Unfortunately, while the sentiment is admirable, it is also misleading. First of all, the metric system is not cool. It's relentlessly mechanical. If the metric system is cool, then so is counting from 1 to 100. The poem goes on to assert that units like inches and feet are boring. But they're not. These English system units are comforting because they are familiar. I admit, however, that I miss the point of the lyric, which is to inspire (or proselytize).

⚘ There are ten millimeters in a centimeter . . . Yes, I knew exactly what my friend was talking about. There are times, after all these many semesters of teaching, when I find myself facing the board with chalk in hand, almost paralyzed with ennui, unsure I can any longer write, "10 mm = 1 cm." I just can't, but eventually I pull myself together and I do.

The reason for my difficulty teaching repetitive and essentially simple information is that it has become so self-evident to me that I don't know what else to say about it. It's as if I'm being told, "Talk about your name." Another analogy is the American who addresses foreigners in English: when they don't understand him, he shouts. And they still don't understand.

What's interesting to me is that even some of the students who "get" the metric system are hesitant to use it. It's like the student of Spanish or French who learns to read and write it but is loath to speak it for fear of sounding funny. In the same manner, I have had students who have accepted and mastered the simple mathematics of the metric system, yet when they do a writing assignment they revert to English units. This is an interesting manifestation of metric anxiety. Sometimes I attribute the relapse to honest exuberance, as with the superb student who was taken with an experiment in which we used electrolysis to separate water into hydrogen and oxygen. She wrote: "We put 100 milliliters of water in the chamber. The water had five grams of sodium phosphate in it. Then we turned on the power. I was, like, wow! And then I thought, hey, we could use this process to make *tons and tons* of hydrogen to solve our energy crisis."

Or take this student who was measuring oxygen output from an aquatic plant: "We marked the measuring tube in millimeters, shined the light on the plant and waited. Finally, after fifteen minutes, the millimeter line moved two inches."

Talk about mixed metaphors.

There are ten millimeters in a centimeter . . .

What my students — and most Americans at large, perhaps — don't know or remember is that there was once a concerted effort to introduce the metric system into everyday usage in this country. I can still recall, back in the 1970s, all those road signs reading, "Think Metric!" which included the speed limit in kilometers/hour. It just didn't take. Americans, despite their alacrity to seize upon new technology, have a visceral disdain for newness when it applies to social engineering, possibly because they fear it will mean new taxes or hikes in existing ones, or that it's communist. This is why it's so hard to get towns and cities to build real bike paths. The result is that in America such projects get done by stealth, and in increments.

For example, American car manufacturers include dual speedometers on their models, to enable the driver to compare miles/hr. to km/hr. And engine capacities are now commonly given in liters. Soda pop has for a long time been sold in liter bottles. This is one of the great success stories: it has become routine for not only young people, but also old fogies, to ask for "a liter of Coke." (Perhaps Coca-Cola should be in charge of America's transition to the metric system.)

Be all this as it may, I don't foresee the advent, any time soon, of the two-liter casserole, the two-deciliter container of heavy cream, or the kilogram bathroom scale. (Although this last might have great appeal, allowing the portly to recite a far more welcome-sounding weight, since there are approximately two pounds in a kilogram. "My weight, doctor? Why, I'm a mere slip of a lad at one hundred kilos.")

There are ten millimeters in a centimeter . . .

My colleague—the one afflicted with aphasia when he thought of the metric system—eventually left the college classroom and went off to teach high school chemistry. He's happy, not only because he's making more money, but because he finds that he is able to teach the metric system with élan, as his fifteen-year-old students are lapping it up and actually using it. I congratulate him.

As for me, it's still a tough slog, made more painful by a haunting dream I recently had. I was lying in the hospital, being prepped for some vague procedure. A generic student of mine appeared in the doorway, holding a plastic bag of fluid aloft. In her other hand she held the IV line and needle. As she approached me she announced, "Here's your liter of morphine, Professor Klose." At which I cried out, "That's milliliter! Milliliter!"

The horror. ✤

the future is now

the new technology

There he sat, lecture after lecture, dutifully tapping away on his laptop with the intensity and devotion of a scribe. But there was one thing I couldn't figure out: if Justin was so assiduous about taking notes, why was he doing so poorly on his tests?

The scales fell from my eyes one day, in the middle of my lecture on the biochemistry of cellular respiration, a rough topic for non-majors. "If there's one lecture you can't afford to miss," I had warned my students the previous week, "it's the next one. Please be sure to attend."

Justin's laptop was open before him, his hands hovering over the keyboard as if he were about to play a Mozart sonata. His girlfriend sat close by his side, gazing at him with stars in her eyes. "All cells have a need for energy," I intoned, and Justin's fingers began to dance. On I went, describing cytoplasmic and mitochondrial events with practiced fluency as Justin clicked away in swift counterpoint. But I feared that, once again, he would do poorly come test time. Why was this? Were typing and comprehending two discrete events, the one performed to the exclusion of the other?

. I reached for one of my overhead transparencies, but it wasn't there. "Excuse me," I said to the class, "I forgot something in my office." I left the room, retrieved the transparency, and returned through the back door. As I passed Justin from behind, I stopped short. There, on his screen, was a lovely blonde posing on a tropical beach, wearing little besides a smile. The thing was, Justin didn't even see me standing over him. But his girlfriend did. She tapped—no, slugged—him on the arm, breaking his trance. He shrugged helplessly and threw me a sheepish smile.

I leaned down to him. "Look," I said. "I was in the Navy, so I appreciate fine art. But it's inappropriate here." Then I pushed his laptop closed. "Get a pen," I said. "And as for you," I continued, turning to his girlfriend, "good choice."

I have always thought of myself as a pretty savvy teacher. I knew where it was at, I knew how to talk to my students, and I felt that they couldn't put anything over on me. I wasn't the new kid on the block. I was widely traveled; I had served on a fighting ship for three years; I was from Jersey.

But despite this, I think I had finally been had. The other day I was chatting with a colleague who has a generous ear. "I've never considered myself naïve," I told her, "but all this time I thought my students were using their laptops to take notes."

She looked at me, threw up her hands and said, "Surprise!"

I now know that students live neither by bread alone nor by every word that comes from the mouth of their biology professor. I find myself competing with Facebook, MySpace, Google,

Hotmail, iPods and text messaging (so that's why so many of my students keep their hands under their desks. I had thought they were just cold). When I appeal to my colleagues for advice or commiseration, they tell me, well, you just have to regulate it, that's all.

But that's not all. The thing is, I don't want to be burdened with yet something else to regulate. I have a twelve-year-old at home, and regulating the use of his GameBoy is like having a second job. I lay down the law, but then find him, long past bedtime, holed up under the covers, clicking away with eyes as wide as a tarsier's.

I realize that the path of least resistance is to just let it go, do my job, recite my lectures and hope for the best. But I can't bring myself to do it. I'd feel as if I were not just giving in, but giving up. When I look at my class and see the text messaging and putative use of laptops for taking notes (although why would someone be smiling—or drooling—while taking notes on the feeding behavior of paramecia?), I bristle. As I tell my students on the first day, "I want you to work as hard for me as I do for you." In other words, we start the course off with a handshake, a word of honor; but many students have little interest in abiding by the bargain.

I found a kindred spirit in another faculty member, a new hire, who had a very uncomfortable run-in with a female student who was text messaging during his instructions on how to prepare an animal blood sample for analysis. The procedure demanded a sterile approach, strict adherence to technique and timing, and careful interpretation of the results. But the student messaged on. "Excuse me," said the prof. "Please stop texting." The student's response: "I will. When I'm done."

The thing that surprises me more than the student's brazen reply was that the teacher was able to get through to her at all, short of whacking her with a two-by-four. And this, at long last, is the point I wish to make: electronic devices in class are not merely diversions, rudely employed, which the student can take or leave. The new technology has little in common with the student of yore seeking momentary respite from a boring lecture by doodling cartoons of the professor in the margins of his notebook. It is, rather, a wormhole into another world: when the students engage their cell phones or laptops or hand-held games, they are briskly transported to a place where I cannot reach them. The result is a temporal amnesia—when they emerge from the trance, they cannot account for what transpired in class during their sojourn in cyberspace. (This is the same thing experienced by people who use their cell phones while driving—they lose track of time and place, sometimes with fatal results when they struggle to return to reality under emergency conditions.)

An example. In my general biology lab I was explaining to my students how to extract and isolate their own DNA (this is way cool) from their cheek cells. The procedure is not complicated, but the steps must be done in the correct order and the reagents must be at specific temperatures. As I spoke to them, one of my students was texting, clearly oblivious to my voice. So I segued into the following monologue: "When I was piloting the space shuttle I was amazed at how easily it handled. My crewmates wanted to try steering, but I said, no, I'm the captain. What a bunch of complainers. Then one of them said it was too hot, that we were flying too close to the sun, so I told him to open a window, and he did. It was very refreshing."

Now, the rest of the class could barely suppress its laughter, but my texting student was still clicking away, her face a grim rictus of intent as she bored laser holes in her device with wide-open eyes. Finally, someone nudged her. She shook her head briskly, as if dispelling sleep, and said, "What?"

"Did you hear what I just said?" I asked her.

"Yeah."

"Well, what did I say?"

Without missing a beat, and still gripping her device, she asked, "Could you repeat it?"

This is where I need to speak up in self-defense by stating that

I am not a Luddite. I use computers (a Mac, naturally). I have a cell phone. And I understand how seductive these devices are. A computer, of course, does more than compute. Consider: e-mail, social networking, movies, the news, dating services, pornography, the power to dig up old classmates who have been anxiously waiting to be contacted by someone they scrupulously avoided in high school; not to mention a website where you can rate your professor for all the world to see. It is clear that no professor, regardless of the subject matter, his electrifying teaching personality, or the dazzling nature of his PowerPoint presentations, can compete with the prospect of a text message materializing in the middle of class with the pressing communication: Hello. (And it gets more dramatic than this: one of my students once received a text message from her boyfriend during a lecture on sharks, stating that he was breaking up with her. When she screamed out, I thought it was my description of the great white that had startled her.)

The inability of students to prioritize their activities—class now, Facebook later—has led not merely to a disheartening degree of incivility, but a general belief that incivility is acceptable, that it is somehow the new wave; or, as one student told me when I asked him to stop talking both to me and his cell phone at the same time: "Civility has changed."

Is it any surprise that I disagree? What that student was saying was that his personal needs trumped everybody else's. This is precisely what a classroom is not about. How can teachers and students promote conversation and a sense of common purpose when there is a prevailing philosophy of every man for himself? Once again, civility is the prerequisite. When one is not civil, one has lost the ability to make the kinds of choices that make the world go 'round. If you come to my class with the expectation of doing well, then ogling porn while I am speaking is not going to dispose me kindly to you come grading time. If you hop out of your seat in the middle of my lecture to take or make a cell phone call, then I will find it more difficult to pay serious heed to you when you need my undivided attention. If you are texting under your desk while I am taking pains to explain a critical concept, I will look on in wonder when you come to my office and ask that I repeat my lecture.

Is all, or any, of this the technology's fault? Of course not. I also don't believe that when a person shoots somebody it's the gun's fault. But the comparison is apt, because both tools are conduits of tremendous power, and both provide for the potential for mayhem. As such, I find myself returning to an idea I had pooh-poohed earlier on: regulation.

Yes. I know. Bad word. But I'm going to use it anyway. Since I cannot make the new technology disappear (nor would I want to, because I like buying books on Amazon and sometimes play Galaga), and I cannot seem to prevail against those students for whom it is a very real addiction, I suppose I must use executive power.

Where shall this power come from? I recently read a short piece in *Newsweek* about some schools that have installed "kill switches" in the classrooms that turn off the wireless signal in those spaces. This solution seems to be at least a stopgap. The professor doesn't need to make repeated speeches about inappropriate uses of tech devices during class, nor does he have to pause to police individual infractors, which can be very uncomfortable or even perilous if a reactive student is involved (remember the old saw about the danger of waking a sleepwalker?). This would shut down the Internet, but would not interrupt cell phone signals. (The march toward larger goals consists of small steps.)

The whole business is, at root, sad. Being in college is very much like love: so many people like the idea of it but are unable to live up to its responsibilities. Likewise, there are many students who like the idea of being in college but struggle with the reality and demands of the learning game.

As I stand at my desk, lecturing away, I am aware of those students who cannot keep their eyes off the clock, willing the minute hand by force of telekinesis to move along. Their efforts are in vain, of course, but they have found the next best thing: devices that allay time and allow themselves to become, in the words of T. S. Eliot, patients "etherised upon a table." The new technology is great stuff, but, like morphine—a useful analgesic—it is addictive. However, unlike morphine, no prescription is necessary, and my students, like students everywhere, have acquired the habit of self-medication.

I'm sure my students have not perceived my frustration, because they still seem to like me and they give me good teacher evaluations. They laugh at my jokes and funny stories about growing up in Jersey City in the 1960s. Some of them are so oblivious to the depth of my antipathy for crapola uses of technology that they occasionally invite me into the vortex. The other day I opened my e-mail to find this subject heading: "Jeannie M. wants you to be her friend on Facebook." I highlighted the e-mail and pressed "delete."

Small steps. ♣

the university of tomorrow

Of all people to ask to take a maiden voyage on the ship of new technology! I still drafted my tests with pen and paper. I owned a typewriter and had stockpiled enough ribbons to last until Armageddon. I corrected my students' papers on cassette tape. And I still lamented the passing of ditto machines.

It was the early 1990s. My university was making its foray into the world of distance education: courses beamed out on closed-circuit television signals. It was viewed as a technology—the "university of tomorrow" — that had to be seized and developed, lest we lose the initiative to other schools.

There was considerable opposition from the faculty, the presumption being that television — already viewed as a malignant distraction and monumental waste of time — was the problem, not the solution. Other faculty simply showed disinterest, hoping, perhaps, that if they ignored so-called interactive television (ITV) it would crawl into a ditch and die.

The university held a number of campus forums to introduce the concept and win converts. I went to a couple of these and was very skeptical about ITV's potential for success. I questioned its suitability for many types of courses, such as foreign languages and laboratory sciences. In addition, there was the problem of accountability: cheating and proxy students taking tests. It seemed, at the time, like a bad, faddish idea.

And then my school asked if I would teach a course over the new system. There was start-up money and special stipends available to prime the pump and get faculty involved. My first response was to gag. But curiosity got the better of me, and before I knew what was happening I was standing before a camera in a classroom — a "send" site — with twenty or so students sitting before me. To my right, behind a window, was a control booth staffed by a technician. The course was Human Ecology and the Future and it would be sent out to ten other sites around the state. A total of sixty-five students had registered. I had my own show.

The thing was, while I had those twenty students sitting in front of me — a valuable prop for orientation's sake — I couldn't see the students at the remote "receive" sites, some of which had only one or two people. But they could see me, of course. This seemed a bit unfair. I liked to stay on top of my students. If they were dozing off or goosing their neighbors, I intervened. In other words, I wanted to insure, to the extent that I could, that my students were paying attention. With ITV, this was impossible. For all I knew, the students who were watching me on the tube were fast asleep, playing solitaire, or shooting spitballs. Or perhaps they weren't there at all.

In consideration of all this, I walked into that first lecture just a bit on edge. There were a few basic things I had to remember: look at the camera, stay in the frame, and ask frequent questions. This last point was important for the sake of inviting the distance students into the classroom conversation. For their part, the students at the remote sites could ask me questions by picking up a phone and calling in, as if they were donating to a telethon. Their disembodied voices came out of a small, flying saucer-shaped speaker on my desk for all to hear. I was alerted to a waiting question by a message scrolled across the monitor. At that point I'd interrupt the lecture by saying something like, "Ah, I see we have a caller on the line."

On that first day the technician was at the ready, sitting in his control booth. As he spun his knobs and clicked his switches, he occasionally threw me a nod, to encourage me, I presume. As I stood there, watching the clock, I kept repeating to myself, like a mantra, "Look at the camera, look at the camera." The whole point was to give the remote students the sense that I was really talking to them, lest they feel marginalized or neglected.

And then, show time. My image popped up on the monitor and, ai-yee! Was that me? No wonder television personalities wore make-up. I looked as drawn and unshaven as Richard Nixon during his debate with JFK. I glanced sidelong at the technician, who waved at me to get on with the program. But I couldn't keep my eyes off the talking head on the monitor, my gaze locked by a combination of vanity and horror. I finally remembered where I was and introduced the material as my on-site students began to scribble away.

After plowing through some introductory information, I asked if there were any questions. Now, in a traditional classroom, the teacher can always tell from the looks in their eyes whether the students are following the lecture. But how could I tell if my solitary scholar sixty miles away in Meddybemps, Maine, had the slightest idea what I was talking about? All I could do was wait a reasonable amount of time for someone to call before moving on with the material.

As it was, not many students called. I came to learn that they had a sort of stage fright about it, because they knew their questions would be broadcast not only to me, but to all the other students at all the other receive sites throughout the state. I remember the first time the phone rang. I gave the go-ahead to the caller, but then, nothing. "Hmm," I prompted. "Are you there?" A few awkward moments later I—we all—heard a stumbling, confused voice, followed by what seemed to be the sound of crying before the caller, whoever he or she was, hung up.

Other callers were not so reticent. One digressed into tales of personal tribulation that had nothing to do with the course (people will say anything to be on TV). Another yelled at me because I tended to use the pronouns "he" and "his" when speaking rhetorically (as in, "an ecologist can do his work in the lab or in the field, as he wishes").

I learned a great deal about the process of distance education on that first day, especially as it compared with the traditional classroom. For example, in my regular classes I could pause, digress, tell an anecdote, or just break down laughing, but in the process keep my finger on the class pulse to see how I was connecting, if at all, and, finally, would pull it all together just as the period was ending. With ITV I had to be more careful, because there was no way of getting a reading on my remote students, and I couldn't use the small number of students sitting before me as an indicator for how the rest of them were doing out there in television land. For example, when making a passing reference to evolution, I made a humorous riff on the age of the earth by saying, in the spirit of Mark Twain, "The earth originated five billion years ago, come November 12th." My on-site students got a kick out of that bit of cleverness. But then the phone rang (it was an angry ring) and when I took the call a woman seemed to lose her mind over what she perceived as my ridicule of divine scripture, even though I had drawn no such comparison. "Well, okay," I responded once her ire had subsided, trying to calm the situation, "this is something that is clearly important to you . . ." Then she hung up. As for me, I moved on, hobbled but still on my feet. (Addendum: that night I received an e-mail from this student, asking if I would like to go out for coffee sometime.)

The show went on. The class was seventy-five minutes long, but by the end of the first twenty minutes I had broken a sweat. Worse, I could see, on the monitor, the sweat stains spreading in my armpits (I had foolishly worn a light blue shirt) like small, expanding river deltas. I found myself watching the clock, wondering what would happen if I finished the material five, ten, or even fifteen minutes ahead of schedule. Tell a story? Ask the students for feedback and wait for the phone to ring? Do a soft shoe?

As the course proceeded, I got better at it. I developed a feeling for pace and timing, and I learned to line up all my notes and overhead transparencies in logical order and in easy reach. For example, in a traditional classroom, if I forgot something, I could excuse myself to retrieve it. But I couldn't create "dead air" while teaching on ITV. And it's still very interesting to me that I actually did get to know my remote students by personality as conveyed by their voices when they called in with questions, as well as the tone and content of the e-mails they sent me after hours. And why not? Blind people, which is what ITV makes of its professors, get to know others just fine and are no less skilled at judging character than those with sight.

Still, I didn't really "know" in any objective way how I was doing. I was, after all, one of the ITV pioneers. How did I compare with other professors teaching over the system? I decided to find out.

I referred to the directory of courses and found a social science course I could spy on. My campus was one of the receive sites, so I wouldn't be disturbing the prof. I went at the appointed time and found two students leaning on their elbows, notebooks open before them. On the screen was a seemingly frozen man who was doing little more than reading the textbook out loud. His lack of animation mesmerized me, and I perched in anticipation of the moment when he would move his hand or look up from his book so that I'd at least know he was alive.

And then I looked at those two students. If not for their elbows holding their noggins up like jackstands . . . well, you get the picture. I came away from that little expedition with few answers or insights. I didn't say to myself, "Shew! I *must* be better than that!" Rather, it got me to wondering again what my remote students were really up to. Were they listening to me? Taking notes? Rolling their eyes at one another? I knew that at least some of them were really there because of their in-class phone calls and the after-hours e-mails that reflected knowledge of what was going on in class. But still . . .

I never got over my doubts about ITV instruction. I think I was competent at it and that my students learned something, but I never became a true believer and certainly didn't put as much muscle into it as some of my colleagues, one of whom actually ventured to teach an anatomy laboratory over the system. When he told me this, my response was immediate: "Are you out of your mind? Just how are you going to do *that*?" Well, he did it. He shipped fetal pigs to all the students, dissected his own pig on screen, and the students mailed their dissected and labeled pigs back to him. These packages were easy to spot: they were the ones leaking formaldehyde.

Be that as it may, I wrapped up the semester with a sense of, "Well, that's over," rather than a whoop of elation at having done a heroic deed. I never taught another ITV course. I'm just not that kind of teacher. I need to breathe the same air as my students, share a good story with people I can hear laughing, and enjoy those moments when I put my hand on a student's shoulder and say, "This is really good work. Really good."

In the interim, ITV is still alive, and the professors who utilize it range from the grandly articulate, knowledgeable, and entertaining to those who could easily be replaced by cardboard cut-outs. But it turned out that ITV is not the university of tomorrow. Other technologies, such as online instruction and podcasted lectures, seem just as effective and are certainly cheaper for the institutions that deliver them.

A few years after my ITV ecology course, I was in a supermarket when a thirtyish woman approached me. "You don't know me," she said, holding an artichoke with all those threatening spikes on it, "but I know you. I had you as a professor on ITV. Human Ecology. I was at one of the remote sites."

Naturally, I had no way of recognizing her, but I thanked her for acknowledging me. And then I asked the question that had been simmering within me all those years. "How do you think I did?"

She touched my arm and said, reassuringly, "You were great. A lot of laughs."

"So you really listened," I said with all the earnestness I could muster.

"Of course. But I was the only one. The others were shooting spitballs." ❦

beginnings

Another school year ends and I am spent. I have almost four months of paid vacation ahead of me — a scandal, I know — but this thought is not enough to rejuvenate me just yet. I feel as if I have been running for eight months and someone, out of the blue, has commanded me to stop.

It ain't that easy.

In truth, once I have given my last final exam there are still a few mop-up sinecures. I literally writhe at my desk as I correct the finals, because there are always a few students who straddle the line between passing and failing. I find myself scouring their grades, their attendance, their class participation, their winning smiles — anything to excavate a point or two to put them over the miserable little top into the passing range.

There are other epilogs as well. The students who missed the final and come to me in search of a make-up. The ones who, finally, get religion and tell me they understand they didn't work very hard but have an abiding sense that the quality of mercy, even in a biology course, is not strained. Those who, flatteringly, want to say goodbye. A couple of requests for letters of recommendation. And, increasingly seldom as I get older, the sweet girl who quietly enters my office, rues her poor performance in the course, and asks if there isn't *something* she can do to pass.

Be all this as it may, the interface between school and no school is still a stark one, and always hard to adjust to. Are these annual endings little glimpses of what retirement holds? When I finally stop teaching for good, will I wake up the next morning and pace the floor? Will I get out of bed at all? Will there be someone chastising me, "For heaven's sake, find something to do with yourself! You're driving me crazy!"

I don't know.

But for now, I do have a comforting ritual that helps me to, as they say, "decompress." I turn my back on my cluttered desk, go home, change, and walk down to the banks of the Penobscot River, which courses behind my home. I take a moment to reflect on something Thoreau said, that when you build a house, build it on the water so that there's one side from which people can't get at you. With this in mind, I push off in my canoe and let the current take me, making only subtle, tentative insertions of my paddle to keep the bow pointed in the right direction.

Now school is truly at my back. The scene before me is so lovely — thickly forested banks, a riverine island, cormorants on the wing — and the silence so absolute that it allows a dirty little secret to bubble to the surface of my thoughts: at year's end, I don't miss school. For eight months my students and I have transited lecture and laboratory and field trip together. I told them stories and they laughed. Some came to my office and cried. I have guided them one-on-one and given what I hoped was good advice. I have met the children of some of the older ones, the parents of some of the younger ones. It sounds like one big, happy family. But all of us know this isn't so, because no sooner does the semester end than they are gone and I am ensconced, alone, in my office. Perhaps the academy is, as we are increasingly told by administrative sages, a business. And so, as with any business, there are times when the doors simply close and everybody goes home.

As the semester wound down and my obligations slackened, I began to reacquaint myself with friends I hadn't hobnobbed with in months. They asked me how I was doing. My invariable response: tired. I am always ashamed to say this because, after more than twenty years of teaching, I feel that I should have the process well in hand and that I should know enough to make things easy on myself so that I am not tired. I am starting to accept that if I have not learned by now how to get my job done without breaking a sweat, I am not going to learn.

As I slip along in my canoe, I come around Ayers Island and

head upriver, against the full force of the current. I do this because it taxes my skills as a paddler and because it is physically strenuous. But it's impossible to travel against the ceaseless rush of water for long, so one must learn to hug the shore, where there are eddy currents that run upriver. I have learned to identify these, and when I hit one, the canoe suddenly slides forward, effortlessly, as if self-propelled. Occasionally I glance back over my shoulder to note the progress I've made.

As true as it is that I am spent by the end of the school year, it is equally true that, as soon as I gain some temporal distance from teaching, the wheels start turning again and I begin to think about September. I'm not yet looking forward to it—those words are too strong—but it's like that first peach-colored glow on the horizon that augurs daybreak: it is a sign that something welcome and familiar is about to happen. I find that I am no longer breathless from running from class to class, assembling lecture notes, setting up laboratories, tracking down misplaced student papers and holding court in my office with those for whom the semester has not gone well. In short, having finally "revved down," I can simply look back at the way I came and then, with renewed clarity of mind, ask myself appropriate questions. How did I do? What could I have done better? Did that new lab on population genetics explain anything or did it simply confuse the issue?

As I ask these questions of myself I already feel a small, preliminary blood surge. I know from repeated experience that by August the semester that lies ahead of me, like that preamble to daybreak, is full of promise. I cannot help but call to mind something that Pliny the Elder said in his *Natural History*: "From the end spring new beginnings."

This thought accompanies me as I reach the end of my trip upriver, the end of my long, hard pull. But rather than allow the current to rush me back down along the same route, I paddle off onto a side branch, where there is also a current, but this time it's flowing my way. It will show me a slightly different riverscape, where I don't know exactly what I will find. I lean forward in my canoe and gaze headlong at my new bearing.

I like beginnings, because they are portals to inevitable surprises. As long as I am open to anything, and have the confidence to know that, after so many semesters of teaching, there is little I feel I can't cope with, the ride should continue to be a good one. The movie *Tadpole*, about a teenager who falls in love with his stepmother, is punctuated with epigrams that periodically flash on the screen. One of these reads, "If we don't find something pleasant, at least we'll find something new."

I couldn't agree more. ⚹